Unshaken

Sally Burke &
Cyndie Claypool de Neve

HARVEST HOUSE PUBLISHERS
EUGENE, OREGON

Cover by Connie Gabbert Design + Illustration

Cover Image © Pearl / Lightstock

Published in association with William K. Jensen Literary Agency, 119 Bampton Court, Eugene, Oregon 97404.

UNSHAKEN

Copyright © 2017 Sally Burke and Cyndie Claypool de Neve
Published by Harvest House Publishers
Eugene, Oregon 97402
www.harvesthousepublishers.com

ISBN 978-0-7369-6973-4 (pbk.)
ISBN 978-0-7369-6974-1 (eBook)

Printed in the United States of America

17 18 19 20 21 22 23 24 25 / VP-JC / 10 9 8 7 6 5 4 3 2 1

What People Are Saying about *Unshaken*

What do you need in these shaky, scary times? Would a different government fix the problems? Governments are made up of fallible humans, and governments never stay in place. Would more money fix things? Money is fleeting and fickle. What about a different job? Employment is capricious and unreliable. What do you need in shaky, scary times? Unshakeable faith. This book masterfully shows us how to live unshaken, even when everything around us quakes and tremors.

Jennifer Kennedy Dean
executive director of The Praying Life Foundation and
author of *Live a Praying Life®* and *Live a Praying Life® Without Fear*

I know this book will deeply bless many, not only here in the United States, but all around the world! Moms in Prayer has been such a blessing—for me personally and for so many others. It has taught many women how to pray in faith and expectation, and how to give God the glory when we see Him answer our cry. To join with other women to pray for our children—there is something beautiful and powerful in that simple action.

Wendy Palau
National Prayer Team, Luis Palau Association

Sally Burke and Cyndie Claypool de Neve have packed this book with the building blocks for a sure foundation so you—and your children—can live unshaken in a shaky world. You will be empowered, encouraged, and equipped to stand sure-footed in your faith with each inspiring story and God's profound and practical wisdom found on every page.

Pam Farrel
author of 45 books including *7 Simple Skills for Every Woman* and
the bestselling *Men Are Like Waffles—Women Are Like Spaghetti*

Unshaken exceeded my expectations! With grace and enthusiasm this book rallies the troops to prayer! There is no condemnation here—only a rousing invitation to receive the unlimited resources waiting at the Throne of Grace, and unshakable emotional, physical, mental, and spiritual stability through prayer. I was enthralled, inspired, and established deeper in Christ through every chapter.

Cheryl Brodersen
host of Living Grace, author of *When a Woman Lets Go of Her Fears* and
Growing Together as a Couple with her husband, Brian Brodersen,
pastor of Calvary Chapel Costa Mesa

How would you like to replace worrying about your children with having confidence and peace? *Unshaken* will not only inspire you to pray for your children, it will teach you exactly how to do it. Even with a busy schedule, you can do this! Praying with a Moms in Prayer group is one of my best commitments.

Arlene Pellicane
speaker and author of *31 Days to Becoming a Happy Mom*

Contents

Part 4: Stories of Unshaken Inspiration

I keep my eyes
always on the Lord.
With him at my right hand,
I will not be shaken.

Psalm 16:8

Foreword

Fern Nichols,
founder of Moms in Prayer International

How grateful I am that the contents of this book will draw you ever closer to your heavenly Father, stirring your heart with a greater passion to know the sovereign, great, and awesome God who hears and answers prayer. The four steps of prayer outlined in this book—praise, confession, thanksgiving, and intercession—will take you to a deeper level of prayer. They will build your faith, helping you to know beyond a shadow of a doubt that there is a God who reigns and that there is nothing He cannot do!

Over 30 years ago, my heart went to anxious fears as I sent my two eldest boys to a nearby junior high school. They were experiencing changing emotions, dangerous temptations, peer pressure, raging hormones, and challenges to their faith. I knew united prayer was the answer to my fears. I cried out to God with one simple prayer: "Lord, who will pray with me?" God answered my one simple, desperate prayer, and the following week five women gathered together to begin to faithfully intercede for our children and their school one hour each week.

I knew this hour had to be used wisely, for we were in a spiritual battle for our children's lives. We needed a strategic prayer plan to counteract the influences of the world, the flesh, and the devil that would rush like a tidal wave against them, intent on destroying them. We needed to stand in the gap for their very lives and the lives of the other children at their school.

This was a time to take action. I formulated the "four steps of prayer" to teach us to pray and to stay focused. When the disciples asked Jesus to teach them to pray, He gave them a beautiful, effective, and strategic way to pray—with the Lord's Prayer. In this prayer, we find the elements of our four steps. The format keeps us "looking up," seeking the Lord's agenda, His mission, His purposes, and His will.

This book is written for any believer who desires to trust God irrevocably and become an effective, confident pray-er. These four steps are used in our Moms in Prayer International groups around the world. They can also be used in your personal quiet time, in family devotions, and in church prayer groups. This book will lead you to the treasures of the four steps of prayer, which have the power to revolutionize your prayer life, deepen your relationship with the Lord, and help you to stand firm no matter what chaos might be swirling around you. The discipline of praying these four types of prayer will keep you in an unshaken place of rest, hope, peace, and joy.

The Lord's Prayer

This, then, is how you should pray:
Our Father in heaven,
hallowed be your name,
your kingdom come,
your will be done,
on earth as it is in heaven.
Give us today our daily bread.
And forgive us our debts,
as we also have forgiven our debtors.
And lead us not into temptation,
but deliver us from the evil one.

Matthew 6:9-13

Part 1

Embracing the Unshaken Invitation

From the Mysteries of Space to the Certainties of Christ

Sally Burke,
president of Moms in Prayer International

With a baby in my arms and a toddler clinging to my leg, I listened to my husband deliver the news that would change our family forever. Ed and I had met while working as engineers on the space shuttle. As handsome as he was, I was attracted to his brilliant mind—and now I was pretty sure he had lost it. As my smart, scientific, and normally sensible husband started to explain how he had accepted salvation in Christ during his morning commute, my life flashed before my eyes.

I was blessed to grow up on the river banks of Cocoa Beach, Florida, a few blocks from the beach. From our beautiful home, I could hear the sea waves crash against the sand, beckoning us to come play. I was raised in a loving family with wonderful parents, two brothers, and a sister, yet we weren't a family of believers, and I lived the way of the world. I sought to fill the superficial desire of worldly lusts.

In whatever I pursued—whether it was sports, academics, or work—I strived for excellence. I loved being a trailblazer, going where few women had gone before, first as one of the few female lifeguards in Cocoa Beach, and later, after graduating from the University of Florida, pursuing a career in the male-dominated space shuttle program. I delighted in my accomplishments and where success could take me. Outside, life was good. But inside, I was filled with uncertainty and a shakiness about what lay ahead.

Even as I drove my new sports car across the country to work as an engineer on the space shuttle in Palmdale, California, daunting questions plagued me. What would tomorrow bring? What was the next goal I should accomplish? And what if I didn't accomplish it? What if I failed?

Once settled into my professional role, I tried to stifle those questions so I could fully embrace my incredible opportunity to work with some of the most brilliant minds in our country—including that handsome, young engineer, Ed, whom I eventually dated and married.

After we had our first of four children, we agreed I'd quit my paying job and replace it with the even harder but much more rewarding job of raising our children. Life was still good, but without God we were walking a self-centered, worldly path. The uncertainty and shakiness continued to grow as I felt the weight of responsibility for the little lives we had brought into the world.

Then came that fateful day when everything changed.

When God Comes into View

Ed came home from work with startling news. On his commute he tuned his radio to Pastor John MacArthur, and for the first time he understood what it meant to be "saved." Right there in the car he accepted Jesus as his Savior. As he explained his decision, I stood there stunned. Was he overworked? Had he lost his mind? Was this going to harm our very comfortable way of life? Why would he rock the boat this way?

Despite my questions and doubts, Ed stayed committed to his new faith in God. Gone was the worldly perspective we had always accepted. In its place was a new, godly one. When Jesus comes into view, everything changes. And over the next several months, my husband *changed*. His thinking was different. He had a new strength from within and a desire to live for God. He knew I was leery of the decision he'd made, but instead of arguing with me or forcing his beliefs on me, he persistently prayed for me.

....

When Jesus comes into view, everything changes.

....

That following Christmas I was expecting one of Ed's usual, wonderful, sparkly gifts. Filled with excited anticipation, I was shocked to unwrap...a Bible. *Really?* I thought. *This is my Christmas present?* As he shared about the care and time he took finding just the right Bible for me, I was intrigued. Since this clearly was a treasure worth far more than any precious stone to him, I decided to read it.

I started at the beginning with the book of Genesis, but it didn't click. So I skipped to Psalms. Wow! As I read the beautiful poetry and the powerful truths stated so simply, I kept thinking that whoever wrote this book was brilliant, like a great calculus professor explaining a difficult concept in a way each student could understand and apply it successfully. God's truth washed over me, opening my eyes to the eternal truth, making me see that the "truth" of the world I had believed was all wrong. I came to an undeniable conclusion: The Bible was truth. Then my husband suggested I read the book of John in the New Testament. Before I finished the first chapter, I knew Jesus was God! I bowed and accepted Him as my Lord.

From Outer Space to Inner Peace

As I began to read God's Word and pray, an anchor to my soul was giving me a great peace. A relationship like no other was being established. The God of the universe was hearing and answering prayer. The truth of God's Word was alive in me. "The sanctifying work of the Spirit, to be obedient to Jesus Christ and sprinkled with his blood: Grace and peace be yours in abundance" (1 Peter 1:2).

As I surrendered my life to God, my priorities shifted. I once had hungered to find ways for humans to reach the stars and the heavens, but now I had an urgency within me to speak intimately with the One who ruled the heavens and the earth. I longed for His peace. I called out to the Lord to teach me to pray. This prayer request would forever change and bless my life. The God who created the universe was listening to me. The answer to this prayer would make an impact not only on my own life but also on the lives of those around me. It would give me the greatest joy of a relationship with my Lord and my Savior. It would be an incredible journey in my walk with the Lord.

God chose to answer this prayer through an invitation from my dear friend Nancy to attend an event focused on how we could pray for our children and schools. It was 1990. That morning we joined many other moms to hear ministering words from Fern Nichols, who founded Moms in Prayer International (then Moms In Touch) in 1984. Fern's powerful words about prayer sank deep into my heart. I left that event profoundly changed by the realization that my children's lives could be blessed through prayer. They could find favor in their teachers' eyes and grow in their relationship with Christ.

My eldest was going to first grade. I was sending him off to a school I had no control over, and, for the first time, I wasn't in charge of his day, his friends, his lessons, or his influences. With all the horrifying news we hear and see happening in our schools, affecting the lives of children, I was motivated to learn more about praying for my kids. I didn't even think about the fact that I had never prayed out loud or been taught how to pray. All I thought about was that my children needed my prayer.

Through biblical, intercessory prayer, the power of God moves profoundly in the lives of those for whom we pray. I desperately wanted God to intervene on behalf of my children and their school. As I stepped into my very first Moms in Prayer group, the women lovingly welcomed me. Though I didn't utter a prayer for the entire hour, I felt accepted. When I realized we would follow four simple steps of prayer, I was relieved and my self-consciousness began to fade. I could feel the presence of God powerfully in that room as we praised Him—me in my heart and the others out loud through His Word, the Holy Bible. Each step was as powerful as the first. Praise was followed by a time of silent confession, then thanking God for answered prayer (talk about a Holy Spirit party!), followed by praying scriptures and praying specifically for our children and then each child's school.

....

Through biblical, intercessory prayer, the
power of God moves profoundly in the
lives of those for whom we pray.

....

Even though I never spoke a word, I felt God lifting my spirit as I gave Him my worries. He replaced those worries with His peace that passes all human comprehension, just as He promises in Philippians 4:6-7. The hour flew by. I knew I would be back the next week! Great peace entered my heart and stayed with me.

The Influence of Mothers' Prayers

God began to stretch our hearts to pray for all the children, not only our own. He answered our prayers so powerfully that even our non-Christian principal and teachers gave us prayer requests. My son's teacher heard I was part of this prayer group and gave me a prayer request for a critically ill student in his class who was not expected to make it through the weekend. Our group lifted him up to our loving heavenly Father. On Monday, I asked the teacher how the student was. She said he was miraculously healed! I was stunned, and the engineer in me wanted to know how, so I asked. I still remember the teacher's confident reply: "It was your prayers!"

When a vice principal left the school for another one, she asked if we could start a group for her new school. At the time, she didn't know the Lord! God surprised and delighted us again and again. During that first meeting, when I, like countless other women, was introduced to Fern's challenge and calling to pray for our children, I knew God was doing something in me. But I had no inkling of how many remarkable happenings He would unfold through the prayers of moms everywhere.

We witnessed revival and spiritual awakening in our elementary school and the schools that surrounded us as other moms came together to pray. We watched Christian students and teachers making an impact on their campuses for Christ and standing up against the world's temptations. Soon I was not only praying out loud, but God was calling me to equip women in my area to exchange fear, worry, and anxiety for the power of prayer.

In 2008 God called me to Moms in Prayer International headquarters, working with women in more than 140 countries. In the most desperate and hopeless situations, I have witnessed God move through women's prayers, making an impact in their communities for Christ. Shaken women become unshaken when they remember the Christ who lives in them is eager to answer their prayers—but they need to ask Him. God has called us to this day and time when our news is filled with terror. Yet we can stand not only unshaken but as women who affect others for Christ.

Shaken women become *unshaken* when they remember the *Christ* who lives in *them* is *eager* to *answer* their *prayers* —but they need to *ask* Him.

For 30 years, I've been studying God's Word and praying God's Word. I have witnessed God transform lives across the globe. I have seen hopelessness, fear, anxiety, and tragedy turn to hope, peace, power, and praise. Women exchange worry to become mighty prayer warriors. They know without a doubt they have been chosen by God to live for Him in His power, strength, and abundance. The stories you will read of Moms in Prayer women are just a few examples of what God is doing in answer to our prayers. These stories have touched my life in a deep and rich way, growing my faith. My prayer is they will also impact your life and grow your faith in a faithful God.

No Greater Adventure

In 2015, Fern Nichols was planning to retire from the day-to-day operations of Moms in Prayer. With the knowledge that I can do all things through Christ who strengthens me (Philippians 4:13), I humbly accepted the request from Fern and the Moms in Prayer board of directors to take up the leadership baton of the international prayer ministry and become president of Moms in Prayer International. I know now, just as I knew then, that I can't do this on my own; I trust in the power of Christ to empower and strengthen me to call women to pray.

Shortly after the announcement, Fern and I were on Dr. James Dobson's radio show. I remember him asking me if I missed the excitement of working on the space shuttle. But truly, nothing compares to the exciting adventure I'm now on, hearing how God is answering prayers and changing lives for Christ. This is the most exciting adventure I could imagine. What a great privilege to be part of a ministry that equips and empowers women around the world to stand unshaken. I'm witnessing women gathering together and making a difference through prayer—transforming their lives, their children, their schools, and their lands. What could be more exciting than that? Others could work on the space shuttle, but this I would not want to miss!

The Secret to the Unshaken Life

With this book, Cyndie—my coauthor and former co-laborer at Moms in Prayer International—and I want to share how to live out the four steps of prayer to remain unshaken in our sometimes crazy world. When we're bombarded with news updates of terrorism, threats of a stock market plunge, and the barrage of media and internet images that run counter to our morals and values, it seems impossible to find peace. Is it possible to rest assured in Jesus Christ, knowing beyond a shadow of a doubt that the promise of Romans 8:28—that He will work everything together for good—is true? Can we truly remain unshaken?

Yes! We can live a faith unshaken and undeterred by anything the world, life, and our own fears present. The secret is found in Psalm 16:8: "I keep my eyes always on the LORD. With him at my right hand, I will not be shaken." Join us on this life-changing journey as we look at how we can incorporate the four steps of prayer—praise, confession, thanksgiving, and intercession—into our daily lives. As we grow in our relationship with Christ through prayer, we begin to develop a life of peace, hope, and trust—a life that can stand unshaken despite the chaos around us. As you deepen your prayer life, watch for God to transform not only your own life but also the lives of your family and those around you.

....

Yes! We can live a faith unshaken and
undeterred by anything that the world,
life, and our own fears present.

....

For Your Unshaken Journey

In this book, Cyndie and I will share biblical truths and practical tips, as well as stories of women from around the globe who have uncovered the secret of standing firm and remaining unshaken through the power of Christ. Throughout these chapters, we'll have full-page quotes to encourage you as you learn to stand unshaken. You're welcome to snap a photo of a quote with your phone to refer back to it during the day, to text to a friend who needs encouragement, or to share on social media (#unshaken). You're also welcome to make a copy of your favorite full-page quote and hang it on your refrigerator, bathroom mirror, or office wall.

Throughout part 2 of this book, you'll encounter Mentor Minutes, which offer more wisdom from Fern Nichols, founder of Moms in Prayer International. We know her insights will bless your journey and encourage each step you take.

Together, we'll explore how to stand firm when faced with the worst, using some of our own personal stories: watching a child wither away because of an illness, experiencing financial distress from a devastating job loss, living with the heartbreak of a loved one serving time in prison. We'll discover truths that lead us to hold on to hope when life seems overwhelming. To help these truths sink in, we suggest working through the companion book *Unshaken Study Guide and Personal Reflections* as you read each chapter. Our desire is that the thought-provoking questions, which can be used individually or as a Bible study in a group format, will help the truths of Scripture take root in your life, allowing Christ to direct your heart to focus on Him, to fill your heart with His peace so you can stand unshaken even in the midst of the scariest times.

1

Living Unshaken in a Shaken World

Truly my soul finds rest in God; my salvation comes from him.
Truly he is my rock and my salvation; he is
my fortress, I will never be shaken.

PSALM 62:1-2

*P*etrified, the young woman took a step forward. With neither a mother nor a father to lean on for guidance, she strived to listen to her godly guardian. He was telling her to go, to step out in faith, but she was frightened. Why her? Why now? What if she was chosen?

The prize for winning this beauty pageant was more than a crown—it was a whole kingdom. And young Esther wasn't sure she wanted to win. After all, she would wind up married to someone she knew only from the troubling stories she had overheard: stories of a king who had banished his wife for not coming when he demanded! Yet the beautiful teen trusted God and followed the path He had set before her. She had no idea at the moment of her feeble obedience that her one action would ultimately save her people from possible extinction.

"Who knows but that you have come to your royal position for such a time as this?" encouraged Mordecai, her guardian and cousin (Esther 4:14). God helped Esther, who was probably no older than a high school freshman, to stand unshaken as she took a bold step of faith to save her people. She told Mordecai, "Go, gather together all the Jews who are in Susa, and fast for me. Do not eat or drink for three days, night or day. I and my attendants will fast as you do. When this is done, I will go to the king, even though it is against the law. And if I perish, I perish" (verse 16).

Did you catch that? "If I perish, I perish." As she stood resolutely in the face of uncertainty, anguish, and possible death, she had no doubt what might be at stake. How does a young woman develop such inner strength? How does she remain unshaken? What was that fortitude that kept her persevering even in the face of possible death for herself and her people?

Her guardian, Mordecai, probably raised her upon the principles presented in Deuteronomy 6:5-7: "Love the LORD your God with all your heart and with all your soul and with all your strength. These commandments that I give you today are to be on your hearts. Impress them on your children. Talk about them when you sit at home and when you walk along the road, when you lie down and when you get up."

Even though Esther was an orphan, her guardian must have so impressed those principles on her heart that at a pivotal moment in history she became a beautiful depiction of Psalm 16:8: "I keep my eyes always on the LORD. With him at my right hand, I will not be shaken."

Esther no doubt kept her eyes on the Lord—dwelling on the promises and attributes of God. As soon as we focus our minds on our heavenly Father, our earthly problems seem so minor in comparison to His might. For Esther, hers were no small problems. She faced an agonizing dilemma of catastrophic significance. And what did she do? She fasted, and called others to fast along with her.

Turning Our Focus to God

What do most of us do when we're stressed? Yep, that's right! As the saying goes, "Stressed spelled backward is desserts." But young

Esther did not call on her ever-willing attendants to find her some delicious morsel. She didn't dive for the ice cream or scour around for chocolate, confiscating the M&Ms out of the trail mix. She didn't collapse on the couch, requesting a glass of wine. She did quite the opposite—she fasted.

....

As soon as we focus our minds on our
heavenly Father, our earthly problems seem
so minor in comparison to His might.

....

The purpose of fasting is to focus all that attention we give to food onto God. Imagine if we did that every time we felt stressed. Imagine if instead of plopping in front of the couch with our favorite Netflix show and a huge bowl of hot-fudge-drenched ice cream, we sat down with our Bibles, pouring out our hearts before the God of all wisdom, letting Him speak to us through His infallible Word. Imagine the peace that would fill our hearts if we called a friend and prayed together over the phone. Or imagine how small our problems would seem if we intentionally began to pray through these four steps of prayer: praise, confession, thanksgiving, and intercession?

As you will discover during our journey together, when we cast our problems in the light of who God is, our once-enormous stresses begin to dwindle in comparison to the size of our great God! If each day we strive to keep our focus on our Creator, then when life's roadblocks and stressful situations come barreling into our path, we will look to the Lord in prayer as our first response, not our last resort.

> I keep my eyes always on the Lord. With him at my right
> hand, I will not be shaken. Therefore my heart is glad
> and my tongue rejoices; my body also will rest secure,

because you will not abandon me to the realm of the
dead, nor will you let your faithful one see decay. You
make known to me the path of life; you will fill me with
joy in your presence, with eternal pleasures at your right
hand (Psalm 16:8-11).

The "right hand" was saved for the place of honor. Even in times
of heart-pounding stress, when we place God first, He makes our
hearts glad and fills us with joy in His presence. And look at the
result in verse 11. He makes "known to me the path of life."

· ·

If each day we strive to keep our focus on
our Creator, then when life's roadblocks
and stressful situations come barreling into
our path, we will look to the Lord in prayer
as our first response, not our last resort.

· ·

Clinging with Confidence

We have seen women in over 140 countries stand unshaken—
some in the face of great danger for themselves and their families.
One day at the Moms in Prayer International headquarters, we
received a call from a surprisingly calm group leader who wanted
to let us know ISIS was invading her land and she was migrating
with her family to a safer location. This mom clung to the truths
she learned through the powerful four steps of prayer (which will
be explored further in part 2). She knew without question that God
would guide her and her family. Even as evil surrounded her, she
was not shaken.

Can you imagine the fear that could have gripped her heart? Yet
she stood confident in Christ's power to overcome. Most of us will

probably never face what Esther did or what the prayer warrior flee-ing ISIS endured. Yet every day provides opportunities to remem-ber to stand firm in Christ.

For me (Cyndie), watching my sister Cathy Chan stand strong despite wave after wave of devastating health news for her husband and her newborn granddaughter was both harrowing and inspiring. She is the one who introduced me to Moms in Prayer and helped me start my very first prayer group. Now, as she boldly allowed friends and family to weather the storms with her, she was a great example of living an unshaken life, with her eyes focused firmly on the Lord.

"My Soul Finds Rest in God Alone"

For Cathy, the ominous potential for death in her family was overwhelming. The heartache was palpable, yet she turned to God with unwavering faith. She meditated on Psalm 62:1-2 many times a day. "Truly my soul finds rest in God; my salvation comes from him. Truly he is my rock and my salvation; he is my fortress, I will never be shaken."

Time and time again, alongside other moms, Cathy had wit-nessed the power of prayer while lifting up the concerns of their public high school and the vulnerable teens navigating a torrential storm of temptations and drama. Then she found herself clinging to those same principles of prayer.

After open-heart surgery, Cathy's husband, Dickson, was cleared, somewhat miraculously, for a kidney transplant. The business owner and father of four boys needed to find a kidney match. Frail and never too far from his dialysis machine, Dickson soon realized the Creator of the universe had been preparing his new kidney since he was a child growing up in Brazil. No one would ever have guessed that his childhood schoolmate, Dave Santos, a Caucasian son of missionaries, would one day be a perfect kidney match for Dickson, a Chinese immigrant to Brazil and then to the United States. Two years after the transplant, Dickson and "Dave the Donor" are both doing extremely well, thanks to God graciously answering the many prayers of friends from around the globe.

Sadly, the potential of losing her husband and watching him waste away as they traveled from doctor appointment to doctor appointment wasn't the only opportunity for Cathy to hold fast to God's promises. Her granddaughter, born to her eldest son, started her life ahead of schedule, bathed in prayer. Because the preemie required so many exams, her retinoblastoma, a rare and often fatal cancer of the retina, was discovered early. Sweet little Ruby and her parents often drive two hours each way to see specialists who keep a close watch on the cancer, aggressively treating any new tumor growth.

Shortly after Dickson's kidney transplant, his dad died suddenly. It was a year that would cause anyone to feel shaken. Through the grief and anguish, the Chan family bonded together. As 2 Corinthians 4:8 declares, "We are hard pressed on every side, but not crushed; perplexed, but not in despair." A few verses later, Paul continues with words of great encouragement. "Therefore we do not lose heart. Though outwardly we are wasting away, yet inwardly we are being renewed day by day. For our light and momentary troubles are achieving for us an eternal glory that far outweighs them all. So we fix our eyes not on what is seen, but on what is unseen, since what is seen is temporary, but what is unseen is eternal" (2 Corinthians 4:16-18).

Following Paul's example in Corinthians is not simple or easy. Some days are harder than others. And that's when we turn our eyes back to God, the author and perfecter of our faith (Hebrews 12:2).

Wait and Watch with Expectation

The Chan family's faith-filled prayers are evident in the spiritual life of Ruby's older brother, Rock. Even at just five years old, he has become quite a prayer warrior. Cathy and Dickson enjoy spending time with Rock when his parents take little Ruby to her oncology appointments a couple of hours away. Cathy shared this story that beautifully illustrates the power of modeling prayer to the next generation. This also serves as a sweet reminder to wait and watch with expectation, hope, and unshakable trust that God will answer our prayers.

On the day we're treating our dear grandson to an outing, I say, "Hey, Rock, Grandpa and I are going to take you over to the pier for a walk. I sure hope we see some dolphins."

Rock immediately starts sincerely praying, "Jesus, I'm asking You that we could see Your beautiful creations today. We would love to see Your dolphins and maybe whales. You have made so many beautiful creatures, and we would love to see them today."

As we park our car, he prays again. "Jesus, it's time. You can open the door and let them go, because we're here."

When we arrive at the beach and start walking on the pier, he prays out loud. "Jesus, You made the beautiful sea creatures. We would love to see a parade of dolphins. We are ready and looking." So of course I'm praying that he won't be disappointed and wondering how we will deal with that if he is—all the while scanning the horizon and begging God to please let us see a dolphin.

Then I spot what appears to be some splashing beyond the waves and tell Rock. We all look, and indeed it is a dolphin. Then we see a few dolphins. And then, I kid you not, by the time we reach the end of the pier, there is a full dolphin parade! There are at least seven dolphins in a line, and they are not just swimming along. No, they are performing. They are jumping and flipping around.

Rock immediately prays. "Thank You, Jesus, for the dolphin parade. Thank You for doing it. Thank You for Your beautiful ocean creatures."

I am dumbfounded. The faith of a little child teaches us so much. In my heart, I pray right then. "Thank You, Jesus, for meeting us at the pier today. Thank You for the beauty of Your creation and for my fantastically spiritual five-year-old grandson and for Dickson's renewed strength and the beauty of the ocean and for Your gorgeous sunset. Thank You for the joy You set in our hearts. Thank You for answered prayers. Thank You for a dolphin parade. I will *never* forget today."

God not only answered the prayers of this young child's heart, but He did so in a way that was truly "more than all we ask or imagine," as it says in Ephesians 3:20. God may be working mightily behind the scenes of your life right now, putting pieces together in ways you've never imagined. But along the way, He delights in giving us "kisses on the cheek"—Moms in Prayer International founder Fern Nichols's description of the sweet encouragement God bestows to encourage us in the midst of longstanding trials. Yet sometimes we miss those sweet "kisses" because we're not looking for them. This big brother of a little cancer patient was looking for glimpses of God's goodness. And our loving Creator showed up in a huge way.

Do You Want to Remain Unshaken?

Both Cathy and Queen Esther struggled with fear and real concerns. But when they set their eyes on the Lord and not on their earthly circumstances, God gave them His powerful combination of strength, peace, wisdom, and clarity. He helped them each stand resolutely, unshaken in the face of death.

God may be
working mightily
behind the scenes of your life
right now,
putting pieces together in ways
you've never imagined.

Do you want to remain unshaken?

Think of that difficult prayer request that knots up your stomach and squeezes your heart. God can answer it in a way that's so
unexpected and better than you could have designed had you tried
to maneuver each one of the pieces. Rest in the truth of Ephesians
3:20-21:

> Now to him who is able to do immeasurably more than
> all we ask or imagine, according to his power that is
> at work within us, to him be glory in the church and
> in Christ Jesus throughout all generations, for ever and
> ever! Amen.

We'll be exploring together how we can use the principles in Philippians 4:4-9 to exchange our fear and gut-wrenching anxiety for
God's inexplicable peace.

> Rejoice in the Lord always. I will say it again: Rejoice!
> Let your gentleness be evident to all. The Lord is near.
> Do not be anxious about anything, but in every situa-
> tion, by prayer and petition, with thanksgiving, pres-
> ent your requests to God. And the peace of God, which
> transcends all understanding, will guard your hearts
> and your minds in Christ Jesus. Finally, brothers and
> sisters, whatever is true, whatever is noble, whatever is
> right, whatever is pure, whatever is lovely, whatever is
> admirable—if anything is excellent or praiseworthy—
> think about such things. Whatever you have learned or
> received or heard from me, or seen in me—put it into
> practice. And the God of peace will be with you.

These words were written by Paul, who continued to rejoice, to
be gentle, to pray, and to maintain the mind of Christ. Even when
he was shipwrecked, thrown in jail, and threatened with death, Paul
wasn't anxious or worried. He poured out his heart to God in both

petition and thanksgiving. And what was the result? A peace mere humans cannot comprehend. Placing our faith and trust in our heavenly Father, allowing Him to be the blessed controller of our lives, results in a peaceful heart, free of worry—a heart that can stand resolute and unshaken.

In the next few chapters, we'll look at the four steps of prayer and how we can, in practical terms, hand our anxiety, fears, and worries to God and allow Him to replace those emotions with His peace that truly "transcends all understanding."

•••••••••••••••••••••••••••••••••

Placing our faith and trust in our heavenly Father, allowing Him to be the blessed controller of our lives, results in a peaceful heart, free of worry— a heart that can stand resolute and unshaken.

•••••••••••••••••••••••••••••••••

Part 2

Praying for an Unshaken Foundation

2

Experiencing the Power of Praise

Be still, and know that I am God;
I will be exalted among the nations,
I will be exalted in the earth.

PSALM 46:10

*I*s your heart pounding with worry? Is your mind racing with fearful "what-ifs"? Is your stomach in a knot over an overwhelming problem? Is the ache of emotional hurt weighing you down? Try moving your eyes off the problems and onto the ultimate Problem Solver. See what happens when you focus on our heavenly Father, who is all-wise and all-knowing; who is trustworthy, faithful, loving, compassionate; who is our Savior, our Counselor, our Provider, our Teacher, our Lord and Master. Suddenly our problems don't seem as big compared to the enormity of the God we serve, the God who loves us and calls us His family. As you begin to learn to praise God, you will be forever changed by His presence and power and peace.

If we immediately begin praising God when difficulties rise, that helps us follow His command.

> Since, then, you have been raised with Christ, set your
> hearts on things above, where Christ is, seated at the

right hand of God. Set your minds on things above, not on earthly things. For you died, and your life is now hidden with Christ in God (Colossians 3:1-3).

And do you remember what Psalm 16:8 tells us will happen when we keep our eyes on the Lord? "I will not be shaken."

••••••••••••••••••••••••••••••

As you begin to learn to praise God, you will be forever changed by His presence and power and peace.

••••••••••••••••••••••••••••••

When most people think about praying to God, they think of handing Him a laundry list of wants and begging Him to bless those requests with a "yes." But prayer is so much more than that. Prayer is our way to develop a deeper love relationship with our heavenly Father, so that when problems come, we can stand unshaken and keep our eyes on Him. We can trust Him and know that He loves us and promises to work all things together for good.

In the four steps of prayer, making our requests and interceding in prayer for others creates the very last step. That way we can first spend time developing our relationship with the Lord and preparing our hearts to hear the Holy Spirit's direction when it's time to intercede. We might come to the Lord in prayer because of a problem or stress, but starting with praise reframes our thinking. As soon as we begin praising God, our thoughts are transformed. We're reminded that we're giving this problem over to the God who created the entire universe. Of course He can take care of it!

Using Scripture to Praise Our Creator

The Bible is brimming with verses describing God's awe-inspiring character and attributes, and it's through these scriptures that we learn to praise God for who He is, for His names, for His attributes, and for His character. Think of the very first verse in the Bible: "In the beginning God created the heavens and the earth" (Genesis 1:1). Out of the breath of His words, our heavenly Father lovingly created every star, planet, and galaxy. He placed them and named them. Yet the Creator of the entire universe also cares about every detail of each one of our lives. He's far greater than whatever situation we're facing, and His care for us is far beyond the reach of our fears.

Do you ever feel as though the earth is giving way beneath your feet, and you're about to be swallowed up by the storm and waves raging around you? Are you drowning in stress, agony, or sorrow? Take time to digest the truths in Psalm 46. As you meditate on this passage, consider what God tells us to do in the midst of the storm.

Psalm 46

God is our refuge and strength, an ever-present help in
    trouble.
Therefore we will not fear, though the earth give
    way and the mountains fall into the heart of the sea,
though its waters roar and foam and the mountains
    quake with their surging.
There is a river whose streams make glad the city of
    God, the holy place where the Most High dwells.
    God is within her, she will not fall; God will help
    her at break of day.
Nations are in uproar, kingdoms fall; he lifts his voice,
    the earth melts.
The Lord Almighty is with us; the God of Jacob is our
    fortress.
Come and see what the Lord has done, the desola-
    tions he has brought on the earth.
He makes wars cease to the ends of the earth.
He breaks the bow and shatters the spear; he burns
    the shields with fire.

> He says, "Be still, and know that I am God; I will be
> exalted among the nations, I will be exalted in the
> earth."
> The Lord Almighty is with us; the God of Jacob is our
> fortress.

Did you catch what our job is during times of stress? "Be still, and know that I am God." We're not asked to help God in any way except to remember that He is our refuge and strength, an ever-present help in trouble. He wants us to rest in the fact that He's got this! Ah, let that wash over you and chase away your stress. Psalm 46 is such a beautiful depiction of what to do when we feel shaken. Remembering God's attributes, character, and names helps us get our eyes off the storms, difficulties, and frustrations swirling around us and onto our capable Lord, who tells us to "be still." Don't you just love that final verse? "The Lord Almighty is with us; the God of Jacob is our fortress."

During harrowing times we must be intentional to praise our heavenly Father. In Lamentations 3, we often focus on God's mercies and compassions being new every morning, but the chapter is filled with pain and angst. Here's a snippet.

Lamentations 3:19-26

> I remember my affliction and my wandering, the bitterness and the gall. I well remember them, and my soul is downcast within me. Yet this I call to mind and therefore I have hope: Because of the Lord's great love we are not consumed, for his compassions never fail. They are new every morning; great is your faithfulness. I say to myself, "The Lord is my portion; therefore I will wait for him." The Lord is good to those whose hope is in him, to the one who seeks him; it is good to wait quietly for the salvation of the Lord.

Despite the author's affliction and bitterness, he intentionally declares, "Yet this I call to mind and therefore I have hope." He remembers who God is—His attributes, His character, and His blessings. And then he transforms his thinking from agonizing to hopeful. "The LORD is good to those whose hope is in him, to the one who seeks him." When life feels as though it's swirling around us out of control, we can stand on this truth: *The Lord is good.*

· ·

We're not asked to help God in any way
except to remember that He is our refuge and
strength, an ever-present help in trouble. He
wants us to rest in the fact that He's got this!

· ·

Let's look at one more passage that shows the intentionality of praising God—especially during times of intense difficulty.

Habakkuk 3:17-19

> Though the fig tree does not bud and there are no grapes on the vines, though the olive crop fails and the fields produce no food, though there are no sheep in the pen and no cattle in the stalls, yet I will rejoice in the LORD, I will be joyful in God my Savior. The Sovereign LORD is my strength; he makes my feet like the feet of a deer, he enables me to tread on the heights.

Imagine there is no food to be had. The grocery stores and farmers' markets are completely empty. You're hungry. Your family is hungry. Your community is hungry. But you shift your eyes from the problem onto the Problem Solver and declare, "I will rejoice in the LORD, I will be joyful in God my Savior. The Sovereign LORD is my strength."

God as Our Refuge Around the World

As I (Sally) sit at my desk, I never know what e-mail or letter might come to me from around the world. With great anticipation, I look forward to what God has in store for us each day as we hear how God is answering prayers around our world. Through the stories of His people, He continues to teach us how to stand with our eyes upon Him, especially in the midst of fear.

One of our Moms in Prayer group leaders sent me her story of victory in Christ. Her town had heard and seen how the Russian tanks had come into Ukrainian towns, pointing their guns at the businesses and then blowing them up. This group leader and her prayer sisters owned businesses. As the enemy tanks started rolling down her street, she was tempted to pack up her family and flee to the hills. However, she felt God calling her to pray instead of run. She and her sisters had been trained to pray through the four steps of prayer, and they started by praising God. These frightened women began timidly, but then they boldly praised God for who He is, acknowledging His power and reminding themselves about His care for them. Do you know what happened? The enemy of fear left them, and they stood strong and unshaken, experiencing both God's peace and His physical protection.

Another woman shared that as she traveled around her country in Africa, training women to pray, she witnessed the power of praise. A group of moms and children was living in a garbage dump to survive after the husbands had been killed by militant thugs. This woman wanted to do so much for these families. While she wished she could provide the resources they needed for an immediate rescue from their circumstances, what she had to give them was the gift of prayer. But she didn't just pray for these fatherless families; she taught them how to pray. The next year, when she went back to check on them, she was astonished to find they were no longer living in the dump, but in apartments. As they learned to praise God for His power, His love, His grace, and His kindness, they began to believe He could move them from the garbage dumps to homes. And He did! The woman who brought them the gift of prayer stood amazed at their faith. They told her with great confidence that they believed Jehovah Jireh, the Lord Who Provides, could provide homes for their families. They took their eyes off their seemingly impossible situation and began to praise the One who can make the impossible possible.

Mentor Minute with Fern

To trust the Lord more, we need to know Him better. "Those who know your name trust in you" (Psalm 9:10). Praising God for His attributes takes us deeper into knowing who He is. To know Him is more than accumulating facts about Him; to know Him is to experience Him in our daily lives in light of who He has revealed Himself to be. When difficult times of suffering, trials, disappointment, brokenness, and hard decisions come, we can "run" to the God we know.

Praise is our greatest weapon against unbelief. Praise dispels the lies of the Enemy, who is constantly working hard at trying to undermine our concept of who God is. When we praise, the Enemy flees!

Fighting the Enemy with Praise

One of our favorite stories about praise is about King Jehoshaphat of Judah, from 2 Chronicles 20. This is one of those true Old Testament stories that makes your mouth drop open. You have to reread it just to make sure you truly understand the miracle God created out of praise. Want to win a battle just by praising God? Check this out!

When King Jehoshaphat first heard about not one, not two, but *three* fierce armies coming to attack Judah, do you know what he did? "Alarmed, Jehoshaphat resolved to inquire of the LORD, and he proclaimed a fast for all Judah. The people of Judah came together to seek help from the LORD; indeed, they came from every town in Judah to seek him" (verses 3-4). When everyone gathered, the king didn't boast about his army, or talk about military prowess, or even discuss a military plan. Instead, he stood unshaken before all of Judah, praying out loud to God.

> LORD, the God of our ancestors, are you not the God who is in heaven? You rule over all the kingdoms of the nations. Power and might are in your hand, and no one can withstand you. Our God, did you not drive out the inhabitants of this land before your people Israel and give it forever to the descendants of Abraham your friend? They have lived in it and have built in it a sanctuary for your Name, saying, "If calamity comes upon us, whether the sword of judgment, or plague or famine, we will stand in your presence before this temple that bears your Name and will cry out to you in our distress, and you will hear us and save us" (verses 6-9).

The king started with praise. But that's not all. There was no doubt in his mind that God would hear and save them. After praising and thanking God, he cried out his request.

> But now here are men from Ammon, Moab and Mount Seir, whose territory you would not allow Israel to invade when they came from Egypt; so they turned away from them and did not destroy them. See how they are repaying us by coming to drive us out of the possession you gave us as an inheritance. Our God, will you not judge them? For we have no power to face this vast army that is attacking us. We do not know what to do, but our eyes are on You (verses 10-12).

Boy, that last sentence is a great prayer! "Lord, we don't know what to do, but our eyes are on You." In struggles at work, with family, at school, in difficult health situations, and in harrowing circumstances like the women in Ukraine and Africa experienced, when we remember who God is, we can stand assuredly in that praise and state, like Jehoshaphat, "Lord, we don't know what to do, but our eyes are on You."

Now check out God's answer to the king—and to us. "Do not be afraid or discouraged because of this vast army. For the battle is not yours, but God's" (verse 15). Don't you just love that? What are you facing today? That battle is not yours; it's God's. Start by praising God for who He is, then rest in the fact that the Creator of the universe is going to take care of your problem!

Jehoshaphat and his comparatively small army are told, "You will not have to fight this battle. Take up your positions; stand firm and see the deliverance the LORD will give you, Judah and Jerusalem. Do not be afraid; do not be discouraged. Go out to face them tomorrow, and the LORD will be with you" (verse 17).

When we remember
who God is,
we can stand assuredly
in that *praise* and state,
like Jehoshaphat,
"Lord, we don't know
what to do,
but our eyes are
on You."

Praise with Every Part of Your Being

What's our part? To show up, resting in complete faith in God Almighty, the Creator of the universe, our Savior and Defender. God says, in essence, "I've got this. I'll battle this Myself, thank you very much. You? You just show up and trust Me." After God shared His plan, the king and all the people of Judah and Jerusalem "fell down in worship before the LORD" (verse 18). Some Levites "stood up and praised the LORD, the God of Israel, with a very loud voice" (verse 19).

The first thing you might notice is that they are *not* shaken. Three big ol' armies are headed their way, and they're totally outnumbered. But what do they do? They cry out praises and a prayer request to God. Their adoration is not just lip service. They fall down to praise Him, and they rise up to praise Him. And God fills them with His peace as they worship Him.

Now, mind you, we have the advantage of reading ahead and seeing what happened. But they didn't. They trusted God purely because He is trustworthy. When their first choice was to praise God, they remembered His power and grace and became unshaken in their faith—even without knowing the whole plan. They had no idea what God's plan was, but they trusted Him and followed His command: "Do not be afraid; do not be discouraged. Go out to face them tomorrow, and the LORD will be with you" (verse 17).

Verse 20 says, "Have faith in the LORD your God and you will be upheld." Guess what weapon of choice they took up to protect themselves: praise songs! "Jehoshaphat appointed men to sing to the LORD and to praise him for the splendor of his holiness as they went out at the head of the army" (verse 21).

How did they remain unshaken in the face of great calamity? They trusted in God and sang praises to Him. Can you imagine what the other armies must have thought if they could hear the small army boldly singing praises to God?

Now comes the completely amazing part. "As they began to sing and praise, the LORD set ambushes against the men of Ammon and Moab and Mount Seir who were invading Judah, and they were defeated" (verse 22). Rival armies began fighting each other, so much so that by the time Judah and Jerusalem reached the battleground, this is what they saw: "When the men of Judah came to the place that overlooks the desert and looked toward the vast army, they saw only dead bodies lying on the ground; no one had escaped" (verse 24). In those days, the winning army took the plunder of the village. And since there was no one else to claim the equipment, clothing, and expensive articles, God blessed His people with them.

························

How did they go from being shaken to
unshaken in the face of great calamity?
They trusted in God and sang praises to Him.

························

Here's how the story ends in verses 27-30:

> Then, led by Jehoshaphat, all the men of Judah and Jerusalem returned joyfully to Jerusalem, for the LORD had given them cause to rejoice over their enemies. They entered Jerusalem and went to the temple of the LORD with harps and lyres and trumpets. The fear of God came on all the surrounding kingdoms when they heard how the LORD had fought against the enemies of Israel. And the kingdom of Jehoshaphat was at peace, for his God had given him rest on every side.

How did they remain unshaken in the face of extremely bad odds? They praised God, not just in words and song, but in action, by following God's orders and taking the step of faith to allow His plan to come to fruition.

Glorify God for What He Will Do

If we could fast-forward time and see God's ultimate plan first, it would be easier for us to stand unshaken. But part of God's plan is for us to learn to trust Him, by setting our eyes and hearts on Christ. And the best way to do that is to start by praising God for His names, characters, and attributes. In the middle of stressful times, begin praising God for as many of these as you can remember: He is loving, faithful, wise, sovereign; He is our protector, our strength, our peace, our Savior.

Finally, think about Mary, a virgin engaged to a godly man. An angel tells her she's going to give birth to a child—God's child. Here is this teen in an era when women who had children out of wedlock could be beaten and stoned. In that situation, most of us would be shaking in our sandals, worrying about what people would think. But Mary wasn't shaken. What does she do when facing this time of uncertainty? She praises God! Spend time meditating on her words of praise to the Lord in Luke 1:46-55. Let them pour over you, filling your spirit with peace and contentment.

Luke 1:46-55

> My soul glorifies the Lord
>   and my spirit rejoices in God my Savior,
> for he has been mindful
>   of the humble state of his servant.
> From now on all generations will call me blessed,
>   for the Mighty One has done great things for me—
>   holy is his name.
> His mercy extends to those who fear him,
>   from generation to generation.
> He has performed mighty deeds with his arm;
>   he has scattered those who are proud in their
>   inmost thoughts.
> He has brought down rulers from their thrones

but has lifted up the humble.
He has filled the hungry with good things
     but has sent the rich away empty.
He has helped his servant Israel,
     remembering to be merciful
to Abraham and his descendants forever,
     just as he promised our ancestors.

What a powerful testimony of faith. Instead of thinking about her immediate circumstances, instead of dwelling on all the "what-ifs" and thinking through various options and outcomes, she praises God, trusting Him completely with her life and the life of her child. Believe it or not, we can do this too. When we move our focus off our problems and onto our loving, all-powerful, sovereign, heavenly Father, then we can have the faith of Esther and Jehoshaphat and Mary. We, too, can remain unshaken.

3

Enabling God's Power Through Confession

If we confess our sins, he is faithful and just and will
forgive us our sins and purify us from all unrighteousness.

1 JOHN 1:9

Unconfessed and unacknowledged sin blocks our clear communication with God. We feel guilty, so we slowly stop praying and reading our Bibles. However, sitting quietly before God and letting Him search our hearts so we can confess our sins is the key to a close relationship with our heavenly Father—and the secret to remaining unshaken when everything around us seems as though it's spinning out of control.

We love the second of the four steps of prayer: confession. We will never, ever be perfect this side of heaven. And our Creator knows that. All those rules and regulations in the Old Testament remind us that we can never be pure enough on our own to enter the presence of the holy and Almighty God. That's why He sent a savior, Jesus Christ, to die for our sins once and for all. All we have to do is admit that we're sinners in need of a savior and ask Him to forgive our sins and come into our lives. That's it! It's a one-time thing. When we become part of God's family, John 10:28 tells us, He will never let Satan pluck us out of His hand.

Daily confession is different from when we first enter the family of God. Once we humbled our hearts to God, asked His forgiveness, and invited Him into our lives as Lord and Savior, we became part of His family, forever and ever. However, to maintain good communication with the holy and perfect One and to be able to hear the promptings of the Holy Spirit, we need to daily examine our lives and see what sin might be clouding our relationship with the Lord. Then we confess it and ask God to give us His strength to refrain from committing that sin again.

Restore Your Relationship with God

In Psalm 32, King David shares a beautiful explanation of how unconfessed sin can ravage our hearts and minds—and how confession restores our relationship with the Lord and erases the agony from our hearts.

Psalm 32:1-5

> Blessed is the one whose transgressions are forgiven, whose sins are covered.
>
> Blessed is the one whose sin the LORD does not count against them and in whose spirit is no deceit.
>
> When I kept silent, my bones wasted away through my groaning all day long.
>
> For day and night your hand was heavy on me; my strength was sapped as in the heat of summer.
>
> Then I acknowledged my sin to you and did not cover up my iniquity. I said, "I will confess my transgressions to the LORD." And you forgave the guilt of my sin.

In Psalm 139:23-24, David shares a prayer that can enhance your daily time with the Lord. "Search me, God, and know my heart; test me and know my anxious thoughts. See if there is any offensive way in me, and lead me in the way everlasting."

....

Confession can restore our relationship with the
Lord and erase the agony from our hearts.

....

David wants God to examine his heart: his attitudes, motivations, desires, and anxieties. Now, that's a bold request! He's asking the Lord to peer into the darkest parts of his life. Our lives might seem put together on the outside, but our hearts can be a dirty mess on the inside. And let's face it, opportunities to sin surround us. In Matthew 5, Jesus explains that not only one's actions but even one's thought life can result in sin. For example, verse 21 and 22 say, "You have heard that it was said to the people long ago, 'You shall not murder, and anyone who murders will be subject to judgment.' But I tell you that anyone who is angry with a brother or sister will be subject to judgment." So, basically, we all sin—a lot!

Emotions themselves are not necessarily sinful, but if we're led by our emotions, we can easily give in to temptation. Picture this: You're driving your car down the street with Christian music wafting through the air. Suddenly another driver comes barreling past you. He's distracted by the phone in his hand and almost swerves into you. You lay on the horn to say, "Hey, I'm here!" And then, out of anger, a series of inappropriate words stream out of your mouth. Now, the fear and surprise are just natural, spontaneous emotions. Not good or bad. Just God-given responses to a near miss. However, when emotions are allowed to take control instead of the Holy Spirit, that can breed sin. And since we're human, those emotions can pop up at any time and become an open door to sin. For example, someone else's good news could quickly bring discontentment and "Why not me?" feelings. That discontentment can breed jealousy, which can lead to gossip and slander and pride.

James 4:1-3 explains it this way:

What causes fights and quarrels among you? Don't they come from your desires that battle within you? You desire but do not have, so you kill. You covet but you cannot get what you want, so you quarrel and fight. You do not have because you do not ask God. When you ask, you do not receive, because you ask with wrong motives, that you may spend what you get on your pleasures.

Unconfessed sin can begin to choke Christ out of our lives. We feel guilty, so we don't have our quiet times. We're disconnected from God, so we begin to rationalize our sins, blaming other people or explaining why our sin should not be considered sin after all. I (Cyndie) used to explain this cycle to my third- and fourth-grade Sunday school classes like this: If you borrowed your friend's toy without asking, broke it, and didn't tell your friend you were responsible, you might become reluctant to hang out with that friend, because when you do you're reminded of what you haven't yet confessed. Because that feeling of guilt can be overwhelming, you begin to avoid that friend altogether in hopes of ignoring that guilt feeling. But what if you went to your friend, said you were sorry, and tried to make amends? One of two things could happen: The friend could forgive you, your guilt feelings would disappear, and your relationship could be restored. Or the person might not forgive you completely, but at least you've cleared the air, and your guilt feelings can begin to subside.

But it's different with God. He promises to forgive us 100 percent of the time and wants our relationship with Him restored. That's a win-win. No sin could ever be so bad that God wouldn't forgive you. First John 1:9 assures us, "If we confess our sins, he is faithful and just and will forgive us our sins and purify us from all unrighteousness."

Mentor Minute with Fern

To pray effectively and with power, we must be clean vessels. That's why confession is crucial to being a prayer force in the kingdom of God. Sin breaks our fellowship with God and with others. Psalm 66:18 tells us if we cherish sin in our hearts, the Lord will not listen. Confession is simply agreeing with God about our sin. We must admit the sin, naming it specifically. Oh, the precious blood of Christ that frees us from the weight and guilt of sin. Oh, the joy of sin forgiven and fellowship with God restored. With clean hands and a pure heart, we draw near to God with boldness and confidence.

Let's not hinder our prayers through unconfessed sin. Let's advance the kingdom of God through powerful, effective prayers that are Holy Spirit directed.

The Sin We Hold On To

Even though we know God will forgive us, sometimes we're reluctant to give up a sin or ask for forgiveness, because, well, we like our sin. We don't want to give it up. Take worry, for example. For parents, there's a sense that worrying about our children is our right. After all, could our children survive without our worrying about their safety, friends, choices, future, and so on? Don't they need us to worry about them? Isn't that part of parenthood? Actually, no. When Paul wrote, "Do not be anxious about anything" in Philippians 4:6, he didn't add, "Except for parents—you go ahead and worry to your hearts' content (or, really, discontent). God needs your help." No. "Do not be anxious about anything" includes our kids.

As hard as it is to imagine, God loves our children even more than we do. How that's possible, we're not sure. But He does. And God looks at their future and sees and knows what He has in store for them specifically. "For we are God's handiwork, created in Christ Jesus to do good works, which God prepared in advance for us to do" (Ephesians 2:10). He knows what obstacles and opportunities will best shape them for that purpose.

Check out what follows the command to not be anxious about *anything*. Philippians 4:6-7 says, "Do not be anxious about anything, but in every situation, by prayer and petition, with thanksgiving, present your requests to God. And the peace of God, which transcends all understanding, will guard your hearts and your minds in Christ Jesus." That is a passage with a remarkable promise—we hand God our worries and anxieties, and He replaces them with His inexplicable peace, a peace not found here on earth. Now, that's a great trade!

Being anxious often feels like a natural part of life—especially if you're a parent. Even though giving up this "right" comes with the promise of God's peace that only He gives and that protects our hearts and minds, we still hang on to our anxieties, fears, and worries. Confession is needed daily—and sometimes several times a day. Confession is clearing the channel between you and God to allow for direct communication with the One who created the entire universe, the One who has a specific plan for you and for each of your loved ones.

Having the Strength to Be Free

Now, you might be thinking, *the sin of worry is nothing compared to my sin*. Maybe God is convicting you of gossiping, or of being jealous, or of being disrespectful to your spouse, or of outbursts of anger. Or maybe of being unfaithful or abusive or stealing or taking drugs not prescribed to you, or of relying on alcohol or food to stifle your anxiety and guilt feelings.

Want to stand *unshaken*?
God's peace needs to
flood our souls.
To do that, we must
confess our worries
and ask God to help us
not continue in this sin.

Often when we're convicted of a sin, we feel like Peter, who realized Jesus was Lord and then blurted out, "Go away from me, Lord; I am a sinful man!" (Luke 5:8). Our sinful nature is repelled by God's holiness, but Jesus Himself tells us in Matthew 11:28-30, "Come to me, all you who are weary and burdened, and I will give you rest. Take my yoke upon you and learn from me, for I am gentle and humble in heart, and you will find rest for your souls. For my yoke is easy and my burden is light."

Carrying around the guilt of sin can be an extremely heavy burden. At our prayer events, we often provide one empty sheet of paper with a big cross printed in the middle. During confession time, we ask each person to sit alone with Jesus and ask Him to expose any sin, as in Psalm 139:23-24: "Search me, God, and know my heart; test me and know my anxious thoughts. See if there is any offensive way in me, and lead me in the way everlasting."

This confession time can be a powerful opportunity to admit our sin, then silently confess it before God. Often we'll have a big wooden cross sitting in the front of the room. We have women write down the sins they're confessing, then—to exemplify God's forgiveness—we each tear up our papers in tiny pieces and lay our sins at the foot of the cross.

On the next two pages, we provide the image of a cross twice so you can sit with the Lord and write down your own confessions on one, and then, on the other, write down your thanksgiving to the Lord for His complete forgiveness. Instead of tearing the confession page out and shredding it, you can lift up the pages in prayer. You can speak your heart and reveal your darkest corners, and then you can celebrate and add to the ways God is speaking forgiveness into your heart and life.

My Confessions

Celebrating God's Forgiveness

At our Moms in Prayer 25th anniversary celebration, one mom finally experienced release from sin that had been plaguing her. Although she had accepted Christ as her personal savior when she was young, in high school she started partying and walked away from the Lord. She married her high school sweetheart, but after a few years of marriage she met another man, and their seemingly innocent conversations at work turned into a short-lived affair. Her husband forgave her, but she had a hard time forgiving herself. Here's what she told us.

My dear husband fought for me, and we started to work on our marriage, rekindling the flame that had blown out. It was a very long and hard process. I remember one night home alone, and the guilt and shame I felt was terrible.

Then a Moms in Prayer leader invited me to attend a local satellite event in the area. I still remember this day so clearly. It came to the time of confession, and we were to get on our knees to confess to God. I cried so hard, and all my guilt and shame that I was living with was gone. I felt at that moment God said, "It is gone; you are forgiven." I felt release and freedom! I went to this event very nervous, but left there feeling forgiven.

Experiencing the Amazing Power of Confession and Forgiveness

One day while I (Sally) was in the Moms in Prayer International office, a woman shared a story with my coworker that left us both in awe of how confession can empower us and propel us forward. Before coming to Christ, the mom had lost custody of her three children. But then she began praying for her children in a Moms in Prayer group. Even though she didn't know where her children were—she couldn't hug them or laugh with them or take care of them—she was confident that through her prayers, God was holding her children close. She thanked God for her Moms in Prayer group, which stood with her without judgment. This mom was not allowing her sins of the past to hold her captive or hinder her ability to impact her future. She was living out Philippians 3:13-15: "*One* thing *I do*: Forgetting what is behind and straining toward what is ahead, I press on toward the goal to win the prize for which God has called me heavenward in Christ Jesus" (emphasis mine). If you look behind you, you miss out on today and cannot impact your tomorrows. Yet, if you pray today, you can impact generations to come.

Letting Go of Unforgiveness

In confession we must let go of the sin of unforgiveness. When the Lord taught His disciples to pray, He emphasized forgiveness as an important part of prayer. Matthew 6:12 says, "And forgive us our debts, as we also have forgiven our debtors."

Early in my time at Moms in Prayer headquarters, I (Sally) had the privilege of working with an amazing volunteer from Rwanda who taught me how to live out this part of confession. When she lived in Rwanda, her first two children were killed during the time of ethnic cleansing. She moved to the United States, had two more children, and joined Moms in Prayer, where she began to learn how to pray for her children with other women. Surrounded by other prayer warriors praying through the four steps of prayer, this mom learned to confess her lack of forgiveness and then to forgive those who had taken the lives of her children. She did not allow the sins of others to shake her. In fact, she went back to Rwanda many times to share this life-changing ministry of prayer, even bringing her children with her. Now her nation is being impacted through prayer. A few years later, one of the key leaders in that country told me with great confidence: "Our nation of Rwanda will no longer be known as a nation of genocide but a nation of prayer!"

Throughout Africa, tribes that once fought against one another are now praying together, bringing peace to their communities. Eastern and Western Europe have experienced centuries of fighting. Even though they have opened borders, the hearts of their people have been closed by sins of the past. Yet many of them are repenting and forgiving, and we are seeing unity through prayer take place. I had the privilege of meeting with a praying group in France, where one woman was a Mennonite, one a Catholic, and the other a charismatic. Instead of holding on to past divisions along denominational lines, they stood together in prayer.

Can you imagine if people of different races, denominations, backgrounds, and expectations would forgive one another and pray together? How much more could we impact these lands for Christ through prayer?

Our Role in the Healing

God wants to free us of our sin. But what's our part? We must confess and hand our filth to God so He can replace it with His peace. Sometimes we feel as though we're confessing when we're actually just making self-deprecating statements. "Why did I tell that questionable joke to my boss—I am such an idiot." Or "I cannot believe I said that to the teacher—I'm so mean." Beating up ourselves mentally might feel holy, but it's not. If you sinned, confess it to God. If you acted mean to the teacher or were inappropriate to your boss, go apologize. And then...let it go! Don't hang on to the sin or regret. God promises to forgive us.

Psalm 103:10-14

> He does not treat us as our sins deserve or repay us according to our iniquities. For as high as the heavens are above the earth, so great is his love for those who fear him; as far as the east is from the west, so far has he removed our transgressions [sin] from us. As a father has compassion on his children, so the LORD has compassion on

those who fear him; for he knows how we are formed, he
remembers that we are dust.

Don't you just love those verses? No matter what you've done,
God will forgive you. Once you have truly humbled your heart and
confessed your sin, it's forgiven. No questions asked. Yes, God might
convict you to make amends with someone you have hurt. If so, do
that. But do so in humility, peace, and love, knowing God loves you
and has forgiven you.

Sometimes, to avoid the guilt feelings sin births, we begin to
harden our hearts. We don't indulge in self-loathing and wallowing
in our regrets; instead we refuse to admit wrongdoings because of a
false belief that confession shows weakness. We rationalize away the
sin so we can live with our choices. However, when we withhold our
confession, we withhold our hearts from being transformed. Anger
and bitterness can begin to wall us off from God and others, and we
have difficulty experiencing the peace and joy of Christ.

....

Once you have truly humbled your heart and
confessed your sin, it's forgiven. No questions asked.

....

Many a young person has walked away from the church to avoid
feeling guilty over sins they don't want to give up. Romans 12:3
encourages, "For by the grace given me I say to every one of you: Do
not think of yourself more highly than you ought, but rather think
of yourself with sober judgment, in accordance with the faith God
has distributed to each of you."

And check out the verses on either side of the more oft-quoted
1 John 1:9:

If we claim to be without sin, we deceive ourselves and

the truth is not in us. If we confess our sins, he is faithful and just and will forgive us our sins and purify us from all unrighteousness. If we claim we have not sinned, we make him out to be a liar and his word is not in us (1 John 1:8-10).

The Gift of a Humble Heart

Confession can be hard. We don't like having to face our sins. And sometimes we don't want to give up our sins. Yet if we want our prayers answered, if we want to stand unshaken, filled with the peace only God can give, we must allow God to search our hearts, expose our sin, and ask Him to forgive us and help us to stay away from temptation. Daily, we need to ask, "Create in me a pure heart, O God, and renew a steadfast spirit within me," as David did in Psalm 51:10. In Hebrew, the word for create is *bara*, the same word used in Genesis 1:1, "In the beginning God created the heavens and the earth." This emphasizes the fact that only God can create a pure heart. We cannot purify our hearts on our own. Only God can do this for us.

As we die to ourselves we allow the resurrection power of Christ to work through us.

> We have renounced secret and shameful ways; we do not use deception, nor do we distort the word of God. On the contrary, by setting forth the truth plainly we commend ourselves to everyone's conscience in the sight of God...But we have this treasure in jars of clay to show that this all-surpassing power is from God and not from us (2 Corinthians 4:2,7).

God lovingly handcrafted each one of us for a specific purpose. When we confess our sins and create a clear channel between ourselves and our Lord, then God fills us with His power to accomplish His will! Do you want your prayers heard and answered, and to be able to not only stand firm through trials but to also fulfill God's purpose for your life? You must confess your sins to the Lord to prepare yourself to be an empty vessel that can be filled with the Holy Spirit.

Let's look in the Old Testament at Daniel. He had been humbly pleading with God to heal his land and free his people. See why God heard him and responded.

> "Now, our God, hear the prayers and petitions of your servant. For your sake, Lord, look with favor on your desolate sanctuary. Give ear, our God, and hear; open your eyes and see the desolation of the city that bears your Name. We do not make requests of you because we are righteous, but because of your great mercy. Lord, listen! Lord, forgive! Lord, hear and act! For your sake, my God, do not delay, because your city and your people bear your Name."

> While I was speaking and praying, confessing my sin and the sin of my people Israel and making my request to the LORD my God for his holy hill—while I was still in prayer, Gabriel, the man I had seen in the earlier vision, came to me (Daniel 9:17-21).

In Daniel 10:12, the angel Gabriel explains why God sent him to Daniel. "Since the first day that you set your mind to gain understanding and to humble yourself before your God, your words were heard, and I have come in response to them."

Confession is both simple and hard. Humbling yourself and asking the Holy Spirit to examine your heart can feel uncomfortable, but the peace and healing that come afterward will be life-transforming and renewing. Here's the awesome thing: God does not expect us to live like Christ in our own efforts. As the apostle Paul writes in 2 Corinthians 12:9, "He said to me, 'My grace is sufficient for you, for my power is made perfect in weakness.' Therefore

I will boast all the more gladly about my weaknesses, so that Christ's power may rest on me."

God's power is at work within us. Isn't that amazing? What can stand in the way of God using us to our fullest calling? Ourselves! And namely, sin. Yet God's power can help us run away from temptation so the Holy Spirit can work in our lives. Hebrews 12:1-3 is a great passage to memorize and hold close to our hearts.

Hebrews 12:1-3

> Since we are surrounded by such a great cloud of witnesses, let us throw off everything that hinders and the sin that so easily entangles. And let us run with perseverance the race marked out for us, fixing our eyes on Jesus, the pioneer and perfecter of faith. For the joy set before him he endured the cross, scorning its shame, and sat down at the right hand of the throne of God. Consider him who endured such opposition from sinners, so that you will not grow weary and lose heart.

The closer we get to Christ, the more easily we recognize sin in our own lives. Conversely, the more we allow sin to continue without confession, the more our hearts become hardened, and we miss out on all Christ has in store for us. As we confess our sins we die to self and allow more of Christ to complete the mighty work He has planned for each one of us.

· ·

As we confess our sins we die to self and allow more of Christ to complete the mighty work He has planned for each one of us.

· ·

Let's end with one more passage to prepare us for our next chapter on thanksgiving.

> Be very careful, then, how you live—not as unwise but as wise, making the most of every opportunity, because the days are evil. Therefore do not be foolish, but understand what the Lord's will is. Do not get drunk on wine, which leads to debauchery. Instead, be filled with the Spirit, speaking to one another with psalms, hymns, and songs from the Spirit. Sing and make music from your heart to the Lord, always giving thanks to God the Father for everything, in the name of our Lord Jesus Christ (Ephesians 5:15-20).

Remember, you do *not* have to confess in your own strength. Ask the Holy Spirit to help you confess and to stay away from temptation. God's peace is waiting for you on the other side of confession—and His peace is what will help you remain truly *unshaken*!

God's peace is *waiting for you* on the other side of *confession*— and *His peace* is what will help you remain truly *unshaken*!

4

Transforming the Dark Through Thanksgiving

Rejoice always, pray continually, give thanks in all
circumstances; for this is God's will for you in Christ Jesus.

1 Thessalonians 5:16-18

*E*ven during times of frustration, agony, pain, or sorrow, a thankful heart can help our trials feel more bearable and less overpowering and faith-shaking. In fact, the mere act of being thankful can transform a grumpy heart into a joyful one. When we start thanking God for our blessings and answered prayers, we're reminded that we serve a big God who loves us and cares about us.

The third of the four steps of prayer is thanksgiving, being intentional to thank God for answered prayers as well as what He is doing in not-yet-answered prayers.

Being Thankful Requires Intentionality

I (Sally) like to think of our thanksgiving prayer time as a Holy Spirit party! When I remember what God has done, specifically for me and my family, my soul begins to rejoice in a sweet and joyous way. At times, I can't help but be thankful. And yet other times I forget the truth in James 1:17: "Every good and perfect gift is from above, coming down from the Father of the heavenly lights, who does not change like shifting shadows."

When my family was shaken by a potential lawsuit several years ago, God taught me what it meant to be unshaken through the power of a thankful heart. I was a stay-at-home mom with four young children, and the legal issues threatened every one of our earthly possessions. Even though we were innocent of any wrong doing, the lawsuit dragged on. I had two choices: I could worry or I could take this situation to God. At the thought of losing what God had blessed us with—however small or big—my eyes were opened even more to all He had provided. Ultimately, we were vindicated, but the long process offered many opportunities to be thankful.

....

When we start thanking God for our blessings and answered prayers, we're reminded that we serve a big God who loves us and cares about us.

....

I began to thank God for our house, for our furniture, for all our worldly possessions. I knew how fast it all could be taken away, and I heard God's voice through 1 Thessalonians 5:16-19. "Rejoice always, pray continually, give thanks in all circumstances; for this is God's will for you in Christ Jesus. Do not quench the Spirit."

Then I realized that the most important thing in my life—salvation—could never be taken away. God has given us our salvation; His everlasting, infinite love for us; our eternal home with Him; His Word; and so much more. This world could destroy or take away all our earthly possessions, yet it could never take God, His promises, and His eternal life from us. During those shaky circumstances, we learned together to stand unshaken through the power of focusing our eyes on Christ and giving thanks for "every good and perfect gift."

We'll all feel shaken at times. That's the very moment when we need to remember the One who is never shaken and whose kingdom stands firm throughout all time. Hebrews 12:28 says, "Therefore, since we are receiving a kingdom that cannot be shaken, let us be thankful, and so worship God acceptably with reverence and awe."

Having a thankful heart can transform even the darkest days. It's a mighty weapon to bless you and those around you with a Holy Spirit party filled with joy! But it's important to note that being thankful is a choice. Do you wake up complaining about the day, or do you wake up remembering the many blessings God has given you? Let us choose to wake up and be thankful! After all, God has already blessed us with all that's necessary. "His divine power has given us everything we need for a godly life through our knowledge of him who called us by his own glory and goodness" (2 Peter 1:3).

Lives Change When Complaining Is Replaced by Thanksgiving

In our Moms in Prayer groups, we endeavor to not talk negatively about anyone. We pray. We always thank God for our teachers and pray for each teacher by name. We know God has placed each one on campus for a reason, and we thank God for the opportunity to pray for all of them.

On my children's campus, one teacher was known to greatly dislike Christians. She was very vocal about this, and it could shake Christian parents who had kids in her class. In Moms in Prayer, we knew we needed to pray for this teacher with a grateful heart. We prayed God would give us opportunity to share God's love with her. As God would have it, this teacher moved to a home across the street from one of the women in our Moms in Prayer group. This teacher saw such joy in her new neighbor she asked this Moms in Prayer woman why she was so thankful and joy-filled. The mom from our group shared about God and invited the teacher to church. The teacher received Jesus along with her whole family. A few years later, I took my two youngest children and placed them in her hands as she became their kindergarten teacher. This now-saved teacher and I would talk about God and prayer. Our prayer group had exchanged grumbling and complaining for thanksgiving and prayer. The result was a teacher and her family coming to know Jesus.

Changing Our Thinking Through Thanksgiving

Intentionally changing our attitude from grumpy to thankful transforms our entire outlook. No wonder God commands us to be thankful. Remember the Philippians 4 verses from the last chapter about exchanging our anxiety and worry for God's peace? Well, check out what's on either side of those verses. Philippians 4:4-9 is a portion of God's Word that lifts our spirits just by reading it. Spend time reading it aloud.

Philippians 4:4-9

> Rejoice in the Lord always. I will say it again: Rejoice! Let your gentleness be evident to all. The Lord is near. Do not be anxious about anything, but in every situation, by prayer and petition, with thanksgiving, present your requests to God. And the peace of God, which transcends all understanding, will guard your hearts and your minds in Christ Jesus. Finally, brothers and sisters, whatever is true, whatever is noble, whatever is right, whatever is pure, whatever is lovely, whatever is admirable—if anything is excellent or praiseworthy— think about such things. Whatever you have learned or received or heard from me, or seen in me—put it into practice. And the God of peace will be with you.

Paul doesn't just tell us to be thankful and rejoice—he explains how to change our thinking. When we're complaining and being critical, what should we let our brains marinate in? Whatever is true, noble, right, pure, lovely, admirable, excellent, or praiseworthy. What most recent thought took up residence in your mind and wouldn't let go? Now take the rubric from Philippians and lay it across your thoughts. What is true? Most often our thoughts are about interactions with people and about what we *think* so-and-so might have thought about us. But do you really know she was judging your clothes? Did he really mean to come across in such a rude way?

Now go back to what is *true*. Go through the list and reframe your thinking. What is noble? What is right? What is pure? What is lovely? What is admirable? What is excellent? What is praiseworthy? Thank God for each of these things and feel the stress and tension melt away.

Recording God's Faithfulness

One thing that can help transform our hearts and minds is keeping a list of all the answered prayers. Prayer journals are great, especially when we go back and record the answered prayers. Often we forget what we prayed for, but looking back at the list and the many answered prayers encourages our hearts. Throughout the Bible, people who were discouraged or frustrated often intentionally recalled God's miracles and blessings. If you need extra help, place reminders of God's goodness around you. Photos and mementos are good "rocks of remembrance." If you have a smartphone, keep a running "note" of thanksgivings, so when you need to transform your thinking, you can easily pull up and review your list.

I (Cyndie) recently had the opportunity to put this into practice—again! God is good at allowing us to have many chances to transform our thoughts into thanksgivings. Have you noticed?

I had just dropped a carload of teenagers off at a birthday party and headed to the grocery store. Now, mind you, this was my first trip to the "real" grocery store after a doctor had added to my ever-growing list of food allergies. I already knew I was allergic to soy, wheat, nuts, bananas, and mint. As my allergies worsened, I learned to read ingredient lists, especially for the soy that hides in almost everything. But now I had been told I was also allergic to corn, oats, dairy, mushrooms, green bell peppers (a random and oddly specific allergy) and, sadly, chocolate.

Discouragement was beginning to overwhelm me as I read ingredients, finding these new allergens hiding in lots of my regular staples. Then I remembered the power of thanksgiving. So every time I found something I could eat, I was especially appreciative. As I woefully passed the Doritos, I thanked God that I would no longer be tempted to overindulge in what I often referred to as my Achilles heel. And I was thankful that perhaps now my allergy symptoms would finally subside.

As I drove away, I saw a teen boy who looked content even though he was using an oxygen tube. While my asthmatic lungs had been tight all morning, at least I had medication to help me. I didn't need an oxygen tank, and there was even hope that soon I'd feel better. And for all that, I was extremely thankful!

Mentor Minute with Fern

Offering prayers of thanksgiving expresses appreciation and gratitude for God's answers. This step reminds us to never take for granted God's gracious answer to our prayers. Even if the answer to our prayers is contrary to what we have asked, our thanksgiving expresses confidence in God's plan, crowding out a complaining, grumbling spirit. Our thanks proclaim that God is a good God, that He can do nothing contrary to His good plan for us. The benefit of giving thanks is priceless—God's rest! The consequences of not giving thanks are frustration and the hindering of our prayers. The simple act of giving thanks allows God to transform us into the image of His dear Son. Let's choose to have an attitude of gratitude, no matter what!

Give Thanks in All Circumstances

First Thessalonians 5:16-18 tells us, "Rejoice always, pray continually, give thanks in all circumstances; for this is God's will for you in Christ Jesus." Give thanks in *all* circumstances. Take a moment to wrap your brain around that one. Do you have health issues? Thank God that He's carrying you through them. Is money tight? Thank God for the provisions He's given to you. Is your house starting to fall apart? Thank God that you have a home to stay in. Are your children driving you crazy? Thank God that you have children and that someday they will grow out of this stage. (And thank God that when the day actually comes that you begin to miss the chaos of this season, you will have sweet memories of His faithfulness to give you comfort and joy.)

Struggles come into all of our lives. Difficulties are part of God's great refining process, used to shape us and to remind us to look to our heavenly Father for wisdom, strength, endurance, and provision. God cares much more about our character than our comfort. In fact, the Bible is filled with examples of people going through agonizing times and yet choosing to thank God for the coming hope.

· ·

Difficulties are part of God's great refining process, used to shape us and to remind us to look to our heavenly Father for wisdom, strength, endurance, and provision.

· ·

The command to "give thanks in all circumstances" was written by a man who had been beaten, imprisoned, and shipwrecked. In 2 Corinthians 11:24-27, Paul provides us with the most incredible example of obedience to this command. Read it and think about the times when you have suffered in the past, or maybe the suffering you're experiencing now.

2 Corinthians 11:24-27

> Five times I received from the Jews the forty lashes minus
> one. Three times I was beaten with rods, once I was pelted
> with stones, three times I was shipwrecked, I spent a night
> and a day in the open sea, I have been constantly on the
> move. I have been in danger from rivers, in danger from
> bandits, in danger from my fellow Jews, in danger from
> Gentiles; in danger in the city, in danger in the country,
> in danger at sea; and in danger from false believers. I have
> labored and toiled and have often gone without sleep; I
> have known hunger and thirst and have often gone with-
> out food; I have been cold and naked.

Despite all he endured, Paul wrote, "I know what it is to be in need, and I know what it is to have plenty. I have learned the secret of being content in any and every situation, whether well fed or hungry, whether living in plenty or in want. I can do all this through him who gives me strength" (Philippians 4:12-13).

Notice that last sentence, "I can do all things through him who gives me strength." *All* things! We do not have to do anything in our own strength—including being thankful. Are you having trouble scrubbing away the cranky, gloom, and pessimism? Ask God to help you. Maybe even start by thanking Him that you haven't had to endure anything near what Paul endured.

Thanksgiving's Abundance—Even in Scarcity

One communist country was so closed off, I (Sally) received updates only when someone personally brought letters to me. Several years ago a woman handed me a note in a Ziploc bag. The people of this communist country didn't have any of the amenities we're used to in the United States. Most didn't have a home phone, much less a cell phone. And they were allowed only one sack of rice per month. On top of that limitation, eggs and milk—even powdered milk—were among a long list of unavailable items that we would call grocery staples. But these women didn't contact Moms in Prayer with a list of needs and complaints. No, they contacted us because they were thankful for God's mighty hand in their country.

In 2004, unbeknownst to us, a mom gave another mom one of our ministry booklets, explaining how to gather moms together to pray through the four steps of prayer for children and schools. Christian moms throughout the area were passing along the power of praying big and bold prayers in this country seemingly closed to Christianity. Seven years later, when we first heard about what God was doing there, the women had just had their first Moms in Prayer event, and 200 women attended!

They wanted to hold another event, but food was so scarce. One mom shared great encouragement.

> Even though they have a shortage of food, the love for the ministry is much stronger. Each and every one of the ladies has been saving one cup of rice per month for several months now, preparing for the big meeting in February. They want to make sure that all who come to the meeting will be able to enjoy a meal and fellowship with one another as they learn.

> I am writing this note to all of you so you may be encouraged that nothing you have done for the Lord will ever return back void; that even a single booklet left in one country has resulted in so much fruit; that when we pray to our mighty God for fruitful results in the countries we are trying to help, expect miracles. That even if we do not receive as much information as we would like to, the Lord is working behind the scenes, and we must trust Him that praying groups are already established and many more are yet to begin.

Today this small country has celebrated its tenth anniversary of involvement with Moms in Prayer and has 700 women participating. Their country is being impacted through prayer.

Life in that country is hard. For moms trying to provide for their children, it's even harder. Now, imagine being a Christian mom, trying to instill a love for Christ in a country that looks down on Christianity. Yet they had hope. They persevered. The whole tone of the letter we received was thankful and rejoicing, without despair. How can we change our perspective like that? Only through Christ. Those moms had "set their minds on things above" and were standing unshaken in the midst of what we would say is extraordinary adversity. They knew they served a living Savior. They trusted Him and thanked Him.

Sometimes I (Sally) will receive letters marked "INMATE" on the envelope from women who participate in one of the prison-based groups. Moms in Prayer has groups in prisons in 40 states, and some facilities have more than one group. These letters are always so precious to me because the incarcerated women have lost so much. They have lost their freedoms, their dreams, and their ability to be with their children—to hold them, to teach them, to hear them, and to share with them. But God is a God who redeems what is lost.

After the women in prison come to know Jesus, they learn how to pray for their children. Wherever we have Moms in Prayer in the prisons, these prisoners are having an influence on the lives of their children through prayer. One prisoner wrote an amazing note of thanksgiving to us. She shared how she was thankful she was caught and placed in prison because it was in prison she found Jesus. She was thankful to God that after she found Jesus, she discovered Moms in Prayer and learned how to pray. She told me she was getting out of prison soon and asked if she could join a Moms in Prayer group once she was out. I rejoiced with thanksgiving because I knew this praying mom would bless many others as she continued to pray for the children and the schools after leaving prison. She chose to be thankful instead of worrying about her children or being bitter and angry about her circumstances. Her heart is full and her prayers are powerful.

Many letters from inmates share how their children have a much higher likelihood of following in their footsteps—engaging in illegal activity and becoming incarcerated. These prisoners could be afraid for or shaken about the future of their children. Yet they are learning to pray and be thankful for all God is doing in their lives and the lives of their children. I see 1 Thessalonians 5:16-18 come alive in them as they learn to pray. "Rejoice always, pray continually, give thanks in all circumstances; for this is God's will for you in Christ Jesus." The secret to a thankful heart in all circumstances is tucked away in a phrase in verse 18: "in Christ Jesus." Remember we can do all things through Christ—even be thankful when it is hard.

Christ as Our Example

Our loving Father knows life can be hard. Jesus experienced the pain of humanity when He walked on this earth. He wasn't born in a clean room with an experienced midwife ready to help Mary deliver Him into the world. He was born in a stinky barn, probably sharing it with a few animals. Later an angel told Joseph to flee with Jesus and Mary to Egypt. Joseph didn't stop to question the angel, didn't stop to pack, and didn't even stop to make a cup of coffee. He immediately obeyed, uprooting Mary and little Jesus, enduring the long journey because he trusted that God had a better plan. We don't know when Joseph died, but as Jesus mourned for Lazarus before raising him from the dead, no doubt Jesus mourned the loss of Joseph here on earth.

Imagine the harassment Jesus received from the Pharisees when He began His ministry on earth at age 30. Then there was the betrayal by His close companions, followed by the flogging and pain He endured even before He was tortured on a cross. There, before dying and rising again, He experienced what must have been the worst pain of all—being separated from God the Father. Jesus and the heavenly Father are one, so imagine the agony of being torn from part of who you are. Imagine all the good and holiness being ripped from you and bearing the burden of every human sin—past, present, and future.

Life can be difficult. Pain is real. We serve a risen Savior who understands our pain. Yet He still asks us to be thankful in all things. He isn't asking us to ignore the pain and sadness—He's telling us to set our minds on Christ. When we look at our struggles through Christ's perspective, we can find a way to live unshaken and with thanksgiving, knowing that even our deepest pain has a purpose when it's held in His hands.

When we look at
our *struggles* through
Christ's perspective,
we can find a way to live *unshaken*
and with *thanksgiving,*
knowing that even our
deepest *pain* has a *purpose*
when it's held in *His hands.*

Thanksgiving Even When Your Heart Is Breaking

If you met Sharon Gamble, you would first sense her sweet and peaceful spirit. Her joy in the Lord exudes from her, but that doesn't mean her life is easy. In fact, she continues to have opportunities to choose between being thankful or sad and frustrated. Yet the lesson she learned about being thankful a few years ago carries her through today's struggles. Here is her story.

It was a dark time for our family. Our beautiful daughter had over-achieved herself into a state of exhaustion and had to leave her college mid-year and come home. She was worn and beaten and in such need of rest and comfort. My mother-heart ached for her and cried out often to God for wisdom in how to help her as she slowly regained strength. I continued to attend my Moms in Prayer group and struggled mightily for a while during the Thanksgiving portion of the hour of prayer. I would hear other moms thanking God for many happy things taking place in their children's lives and wonder what I could possibly pray during that portion. Slowly, God revealed that I had *much* to be thankful for.

Thank You, Lord, that our girl is home with us, where we can see her and hug her and provide shelter for her.

Thank You, Lord, that our daughter is alive.

Thank You, Lord, for the beautiful counselor You brought into our lives, who even makes house calls.

Week by week, thanksgiving by thanksgiving, God revealed how He was at work in the midst of our darkness. I'm not sure I would have seen His hand without those times of thanksgiving in the four steps of prayer. Oh, it is good to give thanks. To notice God's goodness even when it's hard. I will forever be grateful for that season of "hard thanks." It taught me so much and still influences me today as I watch for God's hand every day, through good times and bad.

Giving Thanks Through the Tears

When my (Cyndie's) fifth-grade daughter, Zoe, began withering away before my eyes—losing 12 pounds, sleeping through the day, and enduring great pain in her "hip" (which later was found to be in her colon)—I read Psalm 42 and 43 over and over again. I remember growing up with a song based on Psalm 42:1: "As the deer pants for streams of water, so my soul pants for you, my God." But I didn't know the agony that was attached to those words. As I waited day after day, week after week, and then month after month for my once-energetic child to be restored, healthy, and whole again, Psalm 42 resonated with me. If you read that chapter devoid of any personal heartache, it sounds a bit, well, disturbing. Back and forth the psalmist's emotions go, from pain to remembering who God is and what He can do, then back to pain. Yet that's exactly how I felt. I trusted God. I knew God had a bigger plan. But my heart ached.

I missed my once-active daughter, who had blossomed into such a responsible fifth grader. She used to help the kindergartners with reading, volunteer in the library, and was one of two girls in the whole school who had the honor of folding up the American flag after school each day. Now, Zoe, who always wanted to be out doing something active, couldn't even handle being in the car because it nauseated her. She became a homebody seemingly overnight, and the medical answers came painfully slow. She looked so frail and gaunt and sickly, that when she went for her colonoscopy and endoscopy (which finally diagnosed the colitis) the receptionist assumed she was there to receive blood. And have you ever watched your child be wheeled away on a gurney? Ugh. Heartrending! And the waiting is agonizing. I understood Psalm 42, jostling from despair to hope and back again. See if you can relate.

Psalm 42

> As the deer pants for streams of water,
> so my soul pants for you, my God.
> My soul thirsts for God, for the living God.
> When can I go and meet with God?

My tears have been my food
   day and night,
while people say to me all day long,
   "Where is your God?"
These things I remember
   as I pour out my soul:
how I used to go to the house of God
   under the protection of the Mighty One
with shouts of joy and praise
   among the festive throng.

Why, my soul, are you downcast?
   Why so disturbed within me?
Put your hope in God,
   for I will yet praise him,
   my Savior and my God.

My soul is downcast within me;
   therefore I will remember you
from the land of the Jordan,
   the heights of Hermon—from Mount Mizar.
Deep calls to deep
   in the roar of your waterfalls;
all your waves and breakers
   have swept over me.

By day the LORD directs his love,
   at night his song is with me—
   a prayer to the God of my life.

I say to God my Rock,
   "Why have you forgotten me?
Why must I go about mourning,
   oppressed by the enemy?"
My bones suffer mortal agony
   as my foes taunt me,
saying to me all day long,
   "Where is your God?"

Why, my soul, are you downcast?
>   Why so disturbed within me?
Put your hope in God,
>   for I will yet praise him,
>   my Savior and my God.

That last verse sums up how to have a thankful heart in the midst of pain and despair. Is your soul restless? Spend time meditating on that passage. "Why, my soul, are you downcast? Why so disturbed within me? Put your hope in God, for I will yet praise him, my Savior and my God." When you place your hope in God, you turn your eyes to the Lord. Praise and thanksgiving flow more naturally from a heart that's set on the Lord.

Are You Struggling?

Is life shaking around you? Look to Jesus for your hope and stand on His promises. Are you agonizing over a challenge with a loved one? Remember the promise of Ephesians 2:10, "For we are God's handiwork, created in Christ Jesus to do good works, which God prepared in advance for us to do." Your loved one has a purpose! When my daughter was sick, my thanksgiving was usually that I could trust that God was working all things together for good, as promised in Romans 8:28. And that was my hope. That's what pulled me through, setting my heart and mind on things above, not on things of the earth (Colossians 3:1-2)—looking at today through the eyes of eternity.

There were, of course, little thanksgivings along the way. Each diagnosis was an answer to prayer. We were thankful for that, even if the diagnosis was often scary. Getting in to see just the right specialist—gastrointestinal, rheumatologist, allergist, audiologist—was also an answer to prayer and a specific thanksgiving. Being able to have her transfer to a homeschool program right before it stopped taking more students for the year—also a thanksgiving.

Each little and big answer encouraged us along, reminding us that we pray to a loving and powerful God who delights in answering prayers in surprising ways—in His perfect timing and for the very best outcome. And now, after my daughter racked up a list of diagnoses and was on a string of medications for almost two years, we have the best thanksgiving of all: She's back to her vibrant, energetic self! Her first year of high school, she juggled being on a competitive dance team, in choir, in musical theater, and in gymnastics. All thanks to God!

Are you struggling? God understands. Tell Him your feelings. Ask His help in transforming your heart and mind to be thankful and unshaken. Below is another psalm that echoes our struggling hearts and intentionally focuses on being thankful for past miracles. Walk through this part of Psalm 77 to turn your heart toward thanksgiving.

Psalm 77:8-14

> Has his unfailing love vanished forever? Has his promise
>   failed for all time?
> Has God forgotten to be merciful? Has he in anger
>   withheld his compassion?"
> Then I thought, "To this I will appeal: the years when
>   the Most High stretched out his right hand. I will
>   remember the deeds of the LORD; yes, I will remember
>   your miracles of long ago. I will consider all your works
>   and meditate on all your mighty deeds."
> Your ways, God, are holy. What god is as great as our
>   God? You are the God who performs miracles; you
>   display your power among the peoples.

Psalm 77 goes on to list God's specific miracles. Verse 19 summarizes that even when we don't see God, He is at work. "Your path led through the sea, your way through the mighty waters, though your footprints were not seen."

When fear grips your heart, remember what God has done in the past and thank Him. Let His peace wash over you, as you begin to stand firm and unshaken. As Colossians 3:15 guides and encourages, "Let the peace of Christ rule in your hearts, since as members of one body you were called to peace. And be thankful."

5

Wielding the Secret Weapon of Intercession

You do not have because you do not ask God.

JAMES 4:2

What typically fills you with stress, eradicating the peace of Christ and causing you to be frightened and shaken? Often our peace is shoved out by the force of our worries about loved ones, friends, bosses and coworkers, our country's leaders, our children's educators, those in ministry...and the list goes on. Our frets are futile because we have no control over anyone else's life and how they are affected by decisions, illnesses, and so on. But God does. And through Christ we have a secret weapon of intervening in someone else's life in a positive way. As we lift up our concerns for others to God, we're wielding the most powerful secret weapon: intercessory prayer. As we intercede in prayer for someone, we invite God to intervene in that person's life. And, boy, does He!

The Weapon of Intercession

God commands us to pray—and to pray specifically. Is your child struggling? Is your husband drawn to temptations? Is your coworker in need of knowing Christ as her Savior? Has illness struck a family member? Is a friend going through a breakup? Is a Christian pastor or legislator struggling in his calling? When our hearts are prepared for prayer through praise, confession, and thanksgiving, then we can more clearly hear God's heart and be able to intercede in prayer for others.

As a young believer, I (Sally) learned about the secret weapon of intercession in a surprising way. I had been trying to convince my mom to receive Christ. I tried with my persuasive words, my passion, and my tears. My dad, however, was so intelligent that I defaulted to prayer. It wasn't because I realized the enormous power of prayer at the time; no, it was because I was so young in my faith and wasn't yet sure how to answer his difficult questions. One day I was delighted that my parents were willing to go to church with my family, and I thought my mom might be receptive to accepting Christ there after all my convincing. I thought for sure I had persuaded her, but it was my *dad* who accepted Christ!

I was humbled when I realized prayer isn't supposed to be a last resort; it's to be my first response. This Oswald Chambers quote tells it like it is: "We tend to use prayer as a last resort, but God wants it to be our first line of defense. We pray when there's nothing else we can do, but God wants us to pray before we do anything at all."

Our work of prayer is a great calling. While my words planted seeds for my mom's salvation later, God is the one who draws every person to surrender. Now, instead of worrying about something I have no control over, I pray. And as I pray for others, God transforms them and me at the same time.

Intercessory prayer invites God to intervene on behalf of another. James 4:2 says, "You do not have because you do not ask God." While this is true for our own lives, this is also true when we intercede in prayer for others. Let's look at Philippians 4:6-7 again. These verses command us, "Do not be anxious about anything, but in every situation, by prayer and petition, with thanksgiving, present your requests to God. And the peace of God, which transcends all understanding, will guard your hearts and your minds in Christ Jesus."

We get to exchange all our fears, worries, and anxiety for peace—a peace beyond all understanding that guards our hearts and minds. Don't you want that? We can stand by and worry about our loved ones—or we can pray for them. Second Corinthians 10:4 says, "The weapons we fight with are not the weapons of the world. On the contrary, they have divine power to demolish strongholds." In the face of spiritual and physical battles, prayer is much more effective than worry.

....

We can stand by and worry about our loved ones — or we can pray for them.

....

Every Prayer Is Heard

When my son David was lying in a hospital bed, going into shock because his intestines had just ruptured, I had a choice: I could freak out or I could pray. The Holy Spirit steadied my nerves, and I knelt beside David's bed, pleading with God to heal my child. In the midst of my agony, an inexplicable peace flooded my soul. I knew God heard my prayer. I knew whether God healed David on earth or healed him in heaven, God would accomplish His best plan.

David's gifted doctor was able to operate on him, removing the dead part of the intestine caused by Crohn's disease. They stitched the good parts of his intestines together. Crohn's was a new part of his life, yet God renewed in my son a steadfastness of heart. After he came home from the hospital, David changed the path of success he'd been on. He was reminded that life is short, and this eye-opening truth raises the question, "How will he serve his God while God breathes life in him?"

God Almighty, the One who spoke the heavens and earth into

being, hears and answers our prayers. Isn't that amazing? I just love these prayer promises in Scripture:

- "The righteous cry out, and the LORD hears them; he delivers them from all their troubles" (Psalm 34:17).
- "Let us then approach God's throne of grace with confidence, so that we may receive mercy and find grace to help us in our time of need" (Hebrews 4:16).
- "The LORD detests the sacrifice of the wicked, but the prayer of the upright pleases him" (Proverbs 15:8).
- "The prayer of a righteous person is powerful and effective" (James 5:16).
- "Therefore I tell you, whatever you ask for in prayer, believe that you have received it, and it will be yours" (Mark 11:24).

Think about God's statement in Ezekiel 22:30. "I looked for someone among them who would build up the wall and stand before me in the gap on behalf of the land so I would not have to destroy it, but I found no one." Oh, how we want to be the one who stands in the gap for those we know—and even for those we don't know. Prayer is powerful and effective, and worth every moment of our time when we pour out our hearts to the God who hears on behalf of another person.

Praying like Jesus

Our goal is to live like Christ, and He gave us the ultimate example of a praying life. Reflect on how He interceded for Peter in Luke 22:31-32. "Simon, Simon, Satan has asked to sift all of you as wheat. But I have prayed for you, Simon, that your faith may not fail. And when you have turned back, strengthen your brothers."

Jesus' prayer for all of us is recorded in John 17. Read His powerful words in verses 15 to 21 and spend time contemplating the example He set for us to pray for others and for the world.

John 17:15-21

> My prayer is not that you take them out of the world
> but that you protect them from the evil one. They are
> not of the world, even as I am not of it. Sanctify them
> by the truth; your word is truth. As you sent me into the
> world, I have sent them into the world. For them I sanc-
> tify myself, that they too may be truly sanctified. My
> prayer is not for them alone. I pray also for those who
> will believe in me through their message, that all of them
> may be one, Father, just as you are in me and I am in you.
> May they also be in us so that the world may believe that
> you have sent me.

Christ continues to pray for us. Check out Hebrews 7:25: "He is able to save completely those who come to God through him, because he always lives to intercede for them." Wow, if Jesus continues to intercede for us while He's in heaven, don't you think we should be interceding for others while we're on earth?

Intercessory prayer is such important work that the Holy Spirit helps us.

> In the same way, the Spirit helps us in our weakness. We
> do not know what we ought to pray for, but the Spirit
> himself intercedes for us through wordless groans. And
> he who searches our hearts knows the mind of the Spirit,
> because the Spirit intercedes for God's people in accor-
> dance with the will of God (Romans 8:26-27).

One year at my children's elementary school, our prayer group referenced the yearbook to pray for each child and teacher at the school. God expanded our hearts to pray a big prayer—that all of the children would hear the good news. God answered that prayer and brought to our school a Child Evangelism Fellowship/Good News Club. I was still a fairly young Christian, but I wanted to help, so I volunteered to hand out snacks. After hearing the good news, so many kids wanted to receive Jesus that I was asked to pray with some of them. Oh, those precious children! I looked into their faces—the very children we had been praying for—and they put their little hands in mine as I led them through a prayer of salvation. How amazing to be part of both interceding in a person's life and being used by God to bring that answer to fruition. Today, many of these children are in college and beyond, making an impact on this world for Christ. How blessed I am to play a part through prayer.

....

If Jesus continues to intercede for us while He's
in heaven, don't you think we should be
interceding for others while we're on earth?

....

As I learned to intercede, I witnessed God changing me too! Second Corinthians 3:18 says, "We all, who with unveiled faces contemplate the Lord's glory, are being transformed into his image with ever-increasing glory, which comes from the Lord, who is the Spirit."

Praying in One Accord

Praying alongside another person in one-accord, agreement prayer is powerful. In Matthew 18:19-20, Jesus says, "Truly I tell you that if two of you on earth agree about anything they ask for, it will be done for them by my Father in heaven. For where two or three gather in my name, there am I with them."

The story in Exodus 17:8-13 creates a great visual for agreement prayer. The children of Israel were sent out to battle the enemy. Moses was stationed on top of the hill to intercede for them. He lifted his hands before the Lord. As long as Moses' hands were raised up to the Lord, the children of Israel would win. Yet whenever his tired hands would come down, the enemy would win. His fellow servants of God joined him on behalf of the children of Israel. As it says in Exodus 17:12-13, "When Moses' hands grew tired, they took a stone and put it under him and he sat on it. Aaron and Hur held his hands up—one on one side, one on the other—so that his hands remained steady till sunset. So Joshua overcame the Amalekite army with the sword." Working together, they were victorious.

In Lamentations 2:19, we're told, "Arise, cry out in the night, as the watches of the night begin; pour out your heart like water in the presence of the Lord. Lift up your hands to him for the lives of your children, who faint from hunger at every street corner."

God wants us to be praying for this next generation, our families, our friends, our neighbors, our nation, and so on. But alone we can grow weary and lose heart. We need others to figuratively lift our hands as we pray together in one accord, directed by the Holy Spirit.

When David lay in the hospital bed and his body went into shock because his intestines blew open and sent toxins throughout his body, he was either going home to the Lord or coming back home with us. Kneeling beside his bed, I surrendered my son to the Lord, but I was not alone. My spiritual sisters around the world were praying for him. In fact, while David was still in the hospital, I made it to Dallas that very week to meet with more than 1000 prayer warriors from around the world. My husband and son knew that was the best place for me—praying with these sisters. The women held me and asked me how my son was. When it was announced that he was finally out of the hospital, the room resounded with a great cheer.

Mentor Minute with Fern

What a great privilege to join Jesus in praying the heart of God on behalf of those we love and anyone else God places on our hearts. God's Word, our most important weapon, helps us to pray effectively. His promises are true, and every one of them is backed by the honor of His name. Placing our child's name in a promise of Scripture turns our timid prayers into confident, faith-building prayers. And we stand on tip-toe anticipation expecting a miracle! Isn't it absolutely astounding to think that God's plan involves us in His work through intercessory prayer? Truly we can have no greater ministry, no greater work than to pray for others.

The Gift of Praying Together

Since my children started elementary school, I have been participating in one-accord, intercessory prayer alongside other moms for our children, their classmates, their teachers, the school staff, and the children of the world. I have seen God's miraculous actions as we interceded together. When one is weary or heavy-burdened or has little faith, we're there to lift up her requests to the Lord, just as Aaron and Hur did for Moses. Victory is always waiting as one-accord prayer is poured out before the Lord. I have seen scared, heavy-burdened women transformed into women of courage and peace as they witnessed God answering the prayers of those who were praying alongside them for their children.

So how do we do this thing called one-accord prayer? How do we lift up one another's burdens in agreement prayer? We don't need to talk extensively about the problem. We just start praying. As my dear friend is praying for her wayward child, for example, I listen intently and agree with her in prayer. Then I allow the Holy Spirit to pray through me, often praying for details that hadn't been shared because I receive clarity from the Spirit. We both keep our prayers simple and on the same subject. We pray back and forth, carrying her burden to Jesus, until that subject is covered.

....

Victory is always waiting as one-accord
prayer is poured out before the Lord.

....

One-accord, conversational prayer is short, simple, agreement prayer. My friend might pray, "O Lord, my child has turned his back on You. Help him return." Then I would pray, "Yes, Lord, remove his heart of stone and replace it with a heart after Yours." We would continue praying back and forth about this child alone, until the Holy Spirit led us to pray about another subject. We would move on to intercede for another person, perhaps my own son. I never want to miss out on praying with another person for my family. When someone allows the Holy Spirit to pray through them for someone I hold dear, they're giving an eternal gift to my loved one, and they are giving encouragement and strength to me. Sometimes I have just a mustard seed of faith, because I'm seeing the situation with my own eyes. The pain of the circumstances could be blinding me, but my sister is seeing with spiritual eyes. She's praying with full faith, and that faith is contagious. Many times when I'm asked to pray for someone, I don't know the situation intimately, so I surrender to the Lord and listen intently to the Holy Spirit. The Holy Spirit always knows what is best to pray. He knows the perfect answer too!

We hear about so many answers to prayer that we want to end this chapter with a few testimonies.

Arlene Pellicane: Interceding for Her First Grader

When author and speaker Arlene Pellicane's son was a first grader in a large public school, she joined with other moms to pray for the students and staff—but especially her own child, Ethan.

I wanted to cover his little life in prayer. One meeting, I asked the moms to pray that Ethan would find a Christian friend at school. The very next day, Ethan excitedly told me, "Guess what! I found a Christian in my school." A boy was singing "Joy to the World" and Ethan asked if he was a Christian. He said yes. He not only was in Ethan's class, but he sat right next to him.

My husband, James, felt God's leading to have a weekly after-school Bible club at the school. The moms prayed for direction and open doors. James found a nonprofit to partner with and filled out the necessary paperwork with the school district. After many months of waiting, the club was approved, although our principal was a little hesitant about what other parents might say. We didn't know if anyone would come besides our children to that first club. To our surprise, we had 25 kids that first day! Four years later, we have more than 100 kids on the roster with more than 65 attending each week. The kids sing worship songs in the school auditorium, learn about the Bible, play games, and win prizes. It's been extremely gratifying to see my kids invite their friends. It's given them the experience of inviting others to know about the love of God. Little evangelists can plant many seeds.

There isn't a doubt in my mind that this club was birthed through the intercession of my Moms in Prayer group. Because of their passionate prayers for the lives of kids at my school, we have an open door to share God's love. To top it off, our principal has become one of our strongest supporters.

Our Most Powerful Weapon of All: Prayer

In the jungles of Latin America are a people named after the bugs that swarm their area. Thankfully, God brought the gospel to this village—a village where women were devastated when their children were taken by drug dealers who hid in the jungles. One of our key leaders knew she was called to share the power of prayer with these believing yet hopeless women. As I (Sally) read her report, I rejoiced over God bringing a mighty weapon to these people. When this Moms in Prayer leader began to share the four powerful steps of prayer and how to intercede for their children, the women unfolded their crossed arms and began to wipe tears of joy from their eyes. They kept saying, "We now can see." They knew the hope of the gospel, and now they had learned the power of prayer. They had—and still have—a weapon to fight with, to bring victory against the Enemy and restore life to their children.

I never know who God will bring to share His story with me each day. One afternoon a couple from a communist country came into my office. The husband had grown up as a child of missionaries. His mom's first husband had been killed by villagers. His mom, along with the wives of other fallen men, shared Jesus with killers of their husbands, and many came to know Jesus. After growing up, the man in my office moved back to this communist country as a missionary. There he met his wife, whose parents had been put into jail for their faith in Jesus. When she had been in school, the teachers had challenged her to give up her faith so she wouldn't go to jail like her parents. But she refused. When her own children entered school, she began secretly interceding with other Christian moms for their children and the school staff. Children began coming to know Jesus—and so did some of the teachers and administrators. As tears of joy streamed down her face, her husband commented, "Don't you realize this ministry of prayer is tearing down the walls of communism? The children are understanding the god of communism is not real, but our God is."

Hanaleigh Hazel Kaiser: Intercession Saves a Life

We love to hear answers to prayer—especially from those who were being prayed for. One young adult recently shared how her mom's prayer group and their persistent interceding for her saved her life. At 17, Hanaleigh Hazel Kaiser left her Christian home to move in with her boyfriend. That began a string of physically and sexually abusive relationships, and a spiral into the devastating drug culture, both using and selling methamphetamines.

I was so tired of my life of drugs, sex, and crime, but I could not quit. I felt like there was no way out. As I walked into a room to end my life, I tripped, dropping the syringe and falling on my knees. I was so weak from not eating or sleeping for forty some-odd days that I could not get up. As I was on my knees, I remembered as a little girl seeing my mom lying down prone, flat, face on the floor, crying out to God in prayer. I thought to myself, *I've tried everything else; maybe I can try God.*

I laid down, face to the ground, and really prayed for the first time in five years. I prayed, "God, if You are there, please kill me…or do something." I went to bed that night giving Him time to work. The next morning, I called my parents and asked them to come and get me. I wanted to come home.

Now that I am home, I am better than ever! I attend church, Narcotics Anonymous meetings, and Celebrate Recovery meetings. Now Jesus is real to me. So, moms everywhere, don't quit praying! My mom and her three other Moms in Prayer women—Sudie, Grace, and Judy—are the "angels" who prayed me out of hell!

Today, Hanaleigh has returned to her schooling and is married to a godly man who also had been a prodigal. Together they serve as ushers in their church and are involved in a small group. As she says, "God is good."

Pam Farrel: The Power of Praying Together

Life has not been easy for author and speaker Pam Farrel, yet she continues to stand unshaken. And she has encouraged her children to stand unshaken as well, despite the ups and downs of life.

(Currently she's selling her dream home to spend a year living on a boat so she can be closer to her aging in-laws.) Through each wave of those ups and downs, Pam and her husband, Bill, keep their eyes on the Lord. Here's Pam's story.

I have always been a praying woman. Prayer was the way I coped growing up in a home filled with domestic violence caused by the pain of my father's drinking. Because I wanted something different, something better for our own children, it became natural to pray over each child from the moment I knew God had planted him inside me. As a new mother, one day I held my firstborn son, Brock, in my arms and prayed that he (and all of our future children) might have a strong, stable, unwavering, unshakable faith. One of the lines in that prayer was "Let our children gain the ability to be like a Daniel or Joseph from the Bible, willing to stand alone for their faith if necessary."

Like most moms, when my kids hit those unpredictable tween and teen years, I was concerned about helping them make wise choices in a very unwise world. I was a pastor's wife and led weekly prayer meetings, prayed using a daily prayer journal for our sons, and prayed with my husband each day. Yet I still longed for a circle of moms who cared deeply about their children, their children's school, and their children's future.

While our oldest was in junior high, I knew he would be transitioning from the Christian school my husband oversaw to the local public high school so he could play sports and be a missionary on campus. We had connected him to Fellowship of Christian Athletes, and he was planning on launching an FCA huddle right away. We felt that God was positioning him for leadership as Brock would be trying out for the role of quarterback for the freshman football team.

A friend enthusiastically talked to me about a group of moms

she prayed with every week, so I attended my first Moms in
Prayer meeting. There I found women of faith willing to pray
Scripture for each other's kids and willing to be honest, vulnerable, and courageous. Those women were the prayer support as my
son became quarterback and as he hosted his first party for Christian kids willing to start an FCA huddle. They then prayed for
and worked to support those kids all the way through high school.

Those moms also prayed for Brock as he hosted three "team
parties," where each of his teammates for football, basketball,
and volleyball came for pizza, games, videos, or to hear a professional athlete speak on their faith. They also heard Brock give his
personal faith story and lead them in a prayer so they, too, could
begin a relationship with the God who created them. By the end
of Brock's freshman year, more than 35 of his friends had started
a relationship with Jesus—and some of their moms began to
attend Moms in Prayer, some coming to faith themselves.

Our prayer group prayed that the teens might maintain an
unshakable faith. A few days stand out as vivid answers to these
prayers. As Brock stepped into the role of starting varsity quarterback at age 16, he wanted to make a public statement for his
faith. He called up his buddies on the team and said, "This week,
after we beat Fallbrook, I'm going to the 50-yard line to pray.
Will you join me?" They all said, "We're there for ya, man!"

Bill and I prayed for and with Brock that morning, then my
Moms in Prayer group joined in later. That night, Brock's team
lost 38–0. The guys all just wandered off the field—all except
Brock, who went straight to the 50-yard line. All alone, he knelt
down to pray.

Standing near my husband, I said to Bill, "Honey, he's all
alone. Should I run down and pray with him?" My wise husband said, "Oh, yeah, Pam, that's what the varsity quarterback
wants—his mommy to come rescue him!"

Just then I remembered the prayer we had prayed years ago.

Help him stand alone for You, God. And now he was. *God answers prayer.*

Soon, three players from the *opposing* team joined Brock at the 50, and they prayed. After the game some of Brock's youth leaders from Student Venture and Fellowship of Christian Athletes went down to encourage Brock. Then we made our way to the field.

Reaching up, I took Brock's face in my hands and said, "I have never been more proud of you. I know tonight was one of the hardest of your life—but you kept your word to God."

By Brock's senior year that FCA Huddle had grown to about 200 students, who were all involved at some level. We asked our Brock to preach with his dad on graduation weekend. We encouraged him to share what helped him make wise choices and what helped him walk with the kind of integrity and leadership that garnered him awards, scholarships, and opportunities— that "future and a hope" we moms so often pray for our kids.

One of my favorite lines from that sermon was about Moms in Prayer: "I want to thank my mom and the other moms. Their prayers were like a force field. Those prayers protected me from doing something stupid and gave me courage to stand for truth. Those prayers gave me a vision for how God could use me to influence my peers to know Jesus and the abundant life God offers to all of us if we are courageous enough to say yes to Christ."

Our prayer group also spends a lot of time praying for our children's purity and future spouses. While at college, Brock met his future wife, Hannah, a lovely young Christian woman. *God answers prayer.* Brock is now a football coach and educator, building into teens those same leadership qualities we prayed over him, and Hannah is mother to three children, praying and celebrating the unique wiring of each of our grandchildren. Brock runs optional "leadership" classes at the public high school where he serves as a head coach. These classes are attended by up to 100 young men who are learning biblical values to build a life on. In a society where more than half of all children do not have a father in the home, Brock might be the closest thing to a father these teens will know.

One of our biggest prayers for our family is that we'd leave a legacy of love and that all of us, parents and children, would live unshaken in this world. And God is answering those prayers, one faithful moment after another. We can count on God's *unshakable* character as we pray that we each live and love with unshakable faith.

Pray Continually

As we look at the four steps of prayer, you might be tempted to think this works only for a designated prayer time. Yes, the four steps of prayer create a strategic way to pray with others, helping us remain focused as we pray. But our encouragement is to follow the command in 1 Thessalonians 5:17 to "pray continually." Over the next few chapters, we'll look at how we can integrate praise, confession, thanksgiving, and intercession into our daily lives, so we can transform our shaken fears into unshaken prayers.

As we become women of praise, women of confession, women of thanksgiving, and women of intercession, our lives will be transformed. Our relationship with Christ will be deepened, and—no matter what storms are brewing—we can remain unshaken, living out God's peace and love.

We can count on
God's unshakable character
as we pray that we each
live and *love* with
unshakable faith.

—Pam Farrel

Part 3

Praying with Power and Peace

6

Praying God's Words Back to Him

*This is the confidence we have in approaching God:
that if we ask anything according to his will, he hears
us. And if we know that he hears us—whatever we
ask—we know that we have what we asked of him.*

1 JOHN 5:14-15

What a powerful promise we have in 1 John 5:14-15! God says He will give us anything we ask for. It doesn't say He *might* answer the prayer, or that sometimes He'll say no. It says, "We have what we asked of him." That's 100 percent of the time! Granted, it might not be in our timing, but it's always in God's perfect timing. And the answer is always yes.

But there is one caveat: We must ask *according to God's will*. Ah, now that's the tricky part. How can we possibly know God's will? The only way to truly know God's will is to pray the Scriptures. As it says in 2 Timothy 3:16, "All Scripture is God-breathed and is useful for teaching, rebuking, correcting and training in righteousness."

When I (Sally) was a young mom and a new believer in Christ, I had never actually prayed out loud. So when I stepped into my first Moms in Prayer meeting, I listened. Just listened. For six weeks I prayed along in my heart but didn't say a word. I loved hearing the other women's Holy Spirit–directed prayers for my children. Yet

111

I was too afraid to pray out loud. But after six weeks, I was brave enough to audibly pray the Scripture for my child. The Holy Spirit gave me the courage to speak out His Word, to pray His truth for my son. What a life-changing experience, praying for my son, hearing other moms pray for my son. This was my new top priority for my kids.

God's answers poured out like a flood that first year; our group witnessed dramatic miracles. God healed children of major illnesses. We saw changes in kids' attitudes and behaviors. We prayed that every child would hear the good news, and He brought a Good News Club to our campus. And several teachers at our elementary school accepted Christ as their Savior.

Eventually, I was leading my own Moms in Prayer group. We'd pray for our public school teachers, adapting Acts 26:18: "May [teacher's name] open his/her eyes and turn them from darkness to light, and from the power of Satan to God, so that they may receive forgiveness of sins and a place among those who are sanctified by faith in Christ." One day a mom came into the group upset about a certain teacher. I said, "That's the teacher we're going to pray for today!"

We prayed for that teacher week after week, and God grew our love for her. Soon she came to know the Lord, and my two youngest got to be in her class. I felt so privileged to be able to talk with her about the Lord and about prayer. It was an honor to watch her grow in Christ. But she wasn't the only teacher who became a Christian on that public school campus. Eleven other teachers came to Christ as we prayed Acts 26:18 over them!

Want to see God at work? Pray the Scriptures over the people in your life. How do you know if God is going to answer your prayer? If you pray according to His will, you can be assured of His answer. And His will is the mighty Word of God, which never comes back void. As it says in Isaiah 55:10-11, the Word of God always fulfills His purpose and His plan.

••••••••••••••••••••••••••••••

Want to see God at work? Pray the Scriptures over the people in your life.

••••••••••••••••••••••••••••••

Praying Scriptures for My Son

When I (Cyndie) first became a mom, I prayed over my son, Elliott, asking that he would follow Jesus' words in Matthew 22:37-40. "'Love the Lord your God with all your heart and with all your soul and with all your mind.' This is the first and greatest commandment. And the second is like it: 'Love your neighbor as yourself.' All the Law and the Prophets hang on these two commandments."

So using those verses, this was—and still is—my prayer for my children:

"Lord, may Elliott and Zoe love You with all their heart and with all their soul and with all their mind, and love others as themselves."

A few years ago, as I was reading in the Old Testament for my quiet time, the words of 1 Samuel 2:26 jumped out at me. "The boy Samuel continued to grow in stature and in favor with the LORD and with people." At the time, my son was barely five feet tall and was about to start attending a large public high school. Concerned that his short stature would leave him vulnerable to gangs and bullies, I prayed 1 Samuel 2:26 for him—a lot. "Lord, help Elliott grow in stature and in favor with the Lord and with people." As I shared in the book *When Moms Pray Together,* Elliott's dyslexia caused him to struggle with math, spelling, and reading. Even though he was given an Individualized Education Plan (IEP), I was concerned about his academics. Would he be swallowed up by the rigor of high school? And then I discovered this verse: "Jesus grew in wisdom and stature, and in favor with God and man" (Luke 2:52).

I expanded my prayer. "Lord, help Elliott not only grow in stature and favor with You and others, but help him also to grow in wisdom, just as Jesus grew in wisdom and stature and in favor with You and others." Those verses were so embedded in my mind that the constant prayer of my heart for him became that he would grow in wisdom, stature, and favor with God and others.

But those prayers were not answered immediately. I giggle when I look back at our first visit to meet Elliott's high school counselor. One summer day before he started his freshman year, Elliott woke up with a pinched nerve in his neck and could barely turn his head. Unfortunately, it was the very day we had, weeks in advance, arranged an appointment to discuss high school classes with his counselor. My usually joyful child was mad he had to go anywhere while he was in pain, much less to his new school. In the waiting room, he sat silent and sullen. I was somewhat amused that the other silent and surly-looking teens nodded at him as if they had found a kindred spirit who was equally disgusted that his parent would drag him to school in the middle of summer to register for classes. While I was disappointed Elliott's true personality didn't emerge during that first meeting, I received a good reminder that day to keep praying.

Elliott was coming from a homeschool-based charter school where he was praised for his abilities in video, acting, singing, and drumming. And now he was entering a school where sports were praised and guys who excelled in the arts could be taunted. Yet God gave us a peace about his attending this public school, where he would have extra help for his IEP and where he'd have the opportunity to learn what it means to stand firm for Christ. And so I prayed, and my Moms in Prayer group prayed, and my family prayed. And God answered.

By the time Elliott entered high school, he had grown a few inches, and I thanked God for answering the "grow in stature" part of the scripture. But I continued to pray that he would "grow in wisdom, stature, and favor with the Lord and with people." Along with those verses, I often prayed for my children from Colossians 3:23: "Whatever Elliott and Zoe do, help them work at it with all their heart, as working for You."

Little did I know God would use those prayers together. As Elliott worked "heartily, as for the Lord" (Colossians 3:23 NASB), the teachers noticed, and he began to "grow in favor" with the staff. A couple of months into his freshman year, we attended a college fair. The booths of dozens of colleges were packed with students from all the area schools, yet we heard a sweet voice say, "Hi, Elliott!" It was his school counselor—the one we first met when he looked surly and uninterested. Of the hundreds of students she was responsible for, she knew my son by name. Why? Not because he was having trouble at school (yep, that was my first thought), but because he was polite, friendly, and wore a great big smile.

Often God doesn't show us the answers to our prayer requests so quickly. But God knew I needed the encouragement as we were on this new, somewhat scary adventure called "public high school." And God continued to help Elliott grow in wisdom, stature, and favor. The first time he made honor roll, I didn't believe him until he sent me a photo of his name on the list. And though a great big *D* for freshman Algebra dots his transcript, he went on to excel academically, earning an academic scholarship to attend college.

Even though Elliott was offered drugs his first week of school (he turned them down), he had a strange man try to pick him up as he walked home from school, he was taunted by another student, and he had to stand up to an older student who was fresh out of juvenile hall (they later became friendly), God protected Elliott and truly answered our Scripture-based prayers.

Students with IEPs aren't expected to do well in high school. But as he grew in wisdom—and perseverance—the staff noticed, and he grew in favor in their eyes. He was a great example of God's love shining on the campus and helping him persevere and endure.

Sometimes God Gives the Exact Scripture

Marta Gemelli shared this testimony about God working through an unexpected Scripture prayer.

If I were to look back over 13 years of praying with dozens of women as I moved from state to state and my kids grew through school after school, I find a core focus: praying Scripture. Almost every "God story" is built around praying a scripture verse for my children. I have experienced the fact that the apostle Paul's words to Timothy in 2 Timothy 3:16-17 are true. "All Scripture is God-breathed and is useful for teaching, rebuking, correcting and training in righteousness, so that the servant of God may be thoroughly equipped for every good work."

The most unlikely scripture probably would be the best proof of the power in praying God's Word back to Him. For me, that scripture is Joel 2:12-13. Once a year Moms in Prayer asks the groups to use a common prayer sheet and join conference calls to pray together across the nation. I got on board and printed the prayer sheet for my group so we could pray in one accord with women from Maine to California. But the scripture? *Hmph*.

"'Yet even now,' declares the LORD, 'return to me with all your heart, with fasting, weeping, and with mourning; and rend your hearts and not your garments.' Return to the LORD your God, for he is gracious and merciful, slow to anger, and abounding in steadfast love; and he relents over disaster" (Joel 2:12-13 ESV).

My group was a high school group. Teenagers don't rend their garments. They don't put on showy displays of false humility. They don't display any outward sign of brokenness! I doubted the application of these verses to our children's lives. In fact, I actually prayed in my heart, *Really, Lord? Who chose this?* I prayed the verses for my child, but my heart wasn't in it.

Then we prayed for Jackie (not her real name). Jackie had

been in therapy for over a year. Carol, Jackie's mom, and I placed Jackie's name in the Joel verses: "Lord, help Jackie return to You with all her heart, with fasting, weeping and with mourning; and teach Jackie to rend her heart, not her garments! Help her return to You, her God, for You are gracious and merciful, slow to anger and abounding in steadfast love. Relent over any disaster in Jackie's life."

Even in my weak, doubting mind, God was able to speak. Suddenly, as clear as day, God showed me a picture of Jackie, who self-mutilated through cutting. No amount of therapy was able to break the hurt that caused Jackie to rip at her flesh, week after week.

God showed me that Jackie's cutting was the literal action of "rending her outer garment" or covering—her skin. God didn't want that. He wanted Jackie to rip open her heart to *Him*. He did not want her to rip her skin apart. He was abounding in steadfast love for Jackie. He wanted her heart. The words tumbled out. I wondered if Carol would understand what I was praying. But of course she did. The Spirit guided our hearts and opened our mouths and ears. We prayed in one accord. Up until that time, I didn't know Jackie's cutting was such a deep problem. I knew a little, but not enough to explain how I applied these verses to Jackie's hurt. God was good to show us. When Carol and I finished, we definitely knew God *was* gracious and merciful. He did not want Jackie to suffer as she did.

The way God worked in our hearts—mine and Carol's—was enough. We were convinced of God's great love and concern for Jackie and the fact that the key to Jackie's healing was her walk with the Lord. Even so, we were not prepared for the work God would do almost immediately in Jackie's heart!

The next morning, Carol called. This was strange as we rarely talked on the phone. Stranger yet was the tone in Carol's voice. She *had* to call me. She *had* to share. Jackie had met with her therapist several hours after we prayed together. As they drove home after her therapy session, Jackie shared, "Mom, I'm not cutting anymore. I realized tonight that when I cut, I am letting Satan put his marks on me. I'm not going to do that anymore." And she didn't. She still doesn't! Jackie's words were a miracle and Carol couldn't believe that God worked so quickly after *this* prayer. After this *scripture prayer*. The scripture I found difficult and un-applicable. God is merciful. He is gracious. He pulled Jackie from disaster.

In our weakness, God can be strong. That's what scripture prayer is all about to me. I weakly expect a little progress, a foggy answer, an inkling of God's will. Scripture isn't like that. It is exactly God's will. It is clearly what God wants for His children—that's me and my own beloved kids. Scripture is that road map for how to pray for them. It has taught me to pray bold prayers because He is a bold God and His Word promises bold things. I can pray no less.

Praying God's Word Releases His Power

Often in countries where the spiritual warfare is very apparent, the testimonies are jaw-droppingly bold. As Moms in Prayer International has partnered with mission ministries, women have shared the four steps of prayer with women all over the world. I (Sally) will always remember this story of one of the bravest missionaries I know. She stands a little more than five feet tall, but no jungle, no danger, intimidates her! After a group of women heard the gospel and believed, she taught them how to pray. One of the scriptures she used to teach them to pray for their children was Zechariah 2:5: "'I myself will be a wall of fire around it,' declares the LORD, 'and I will be its glory within.'" One of the young boys, who had a newly praying mom, was snatched by a witch doctor and taken to be sacrificed.

The group prayed from this verse: "May God be the wall of fire around our children and may He be the glory within them." Even though the boy had been drugged and was lying on a table to be sacrificed, he was alert enough to hear one man exclaim, "I can't touch him. It's as though there's a wall of fire around him." The boy got up, ran away, and made it safely home. Authorities were alerted and caught the men who had taken this boy.

Want to enhance your prayer life? Learn the power of praying scriptures.

Your Turn

We'll list a few scripture prayers below, but the Word of God is filled with powerful verses that can be prayed for you and your loved ones. Each day, as you spend time in the Bible, ask God to show you a verse or verses you can pray back to Him—knowing that when we pray God's Word, we're without a doubt praying God's will. Sometimes it helps to look up the verses in other versions of the Bible, since some versions might be easier to pray.

As you pray, remember 1 John 5:14-15. God promises to answer your prayers that are according to His will, in His perfect timing. So be watching with expectation for God's sometimes-surprising answers to your prayers.

Each scripture prayer provided here is adapted from a Bible verse. Simply put in the verse the name of the person for whom you are interceding. In Moms in Prayer, we pray for children, schools, and school staff. But this powerful way of praying can be used to pray for your friends, husband, parents, siblings, coworkers, teammates, classmates, school, or church staff. Ask God for whom you should pray each one of these scripture prayers.

As you spend time in the Bible,
ask God to show you
a verse or verses
you can *pray back* to Him—
knowing that when we
pray God's Word,
we're without a doubt
praying God's will.

Praying God's Word for Others

Most High, through Your unfailing love, I pray _____ will not be shaken. —From Psalm 21:7

Sovereign Lord, give _____ a new heart and put a new spirit in her. —From Ezekiel 36:26

Jesus, I pray _____ will believe in You. —From John 14:1

Lord, show _____ the way of life, granting him the joy of Your presence and the pleasures of living with You forever. —From Psalm 16:11 (NLT)

When anxiety is great within _____, may Your consolation bring her joy. —From Psalm 94:19

I pray _____ will live in harmony with others. —From Romans 12:16

Lord, I pray You will be the light that keeps _____ safe. —From Psalm 27:1 (CEV)

God, will You give _____ more and more grace and peace as he grows in the knowledge of You and Jesus our Lord? —From 2 Peter 1:2 (NLT)

God, I pray _____ will give all her worries to You because You care for her. —From 1 Peter 5:7 (NLV)

God of peace, I pray You work in _____ what is pleasing to You. —From Hebrews 13:21

God, I pray You will give _____ Your Spirit, so that he may know You better. —From Ephesians 1:17

Lord, may Your Word be very near _____, in her mouth and heart, so she may obey it. —From Deuteronomy 30:14

I pray _____ will not let kindness and truth leave him. May _____ tie them around his neck and write them upon his heart. —From Proverbs 3:3 (NLV)

God, I pray You will give more and more grace and peace to _____ as she grows in knowledge of You. —From 2 Peter 1:2 (NLT)

Eternal God, I pray You are _____'s refuge and that Your everlasting arms are under him. —From Deuteronomy 33:27 (NLT)

Lord, in Your light may _____ see light. —From Psalm 36:9

Lord, I pray _____'s soul will glorify You. —From Luke 1:46

Help _____ sing of Your great love forever; may she make your faithfulness known through all generations. —From Psalm 89:1

7

Petitioning on Your Own Behalf

*Three times I pleaded with the Lord to take it away
from me. But he said to me, "My grace is sufficient for
you, for my power is made perfect in weakness."*

2 CORINTHIANS 12:8-9

Want to remain unshaken through times of trial? Learn to pray for yourself as well as for others.

If you're like me (Cyndie), however, you find it easier to pray for others—praying for strength, wisdom, clarity, peace, and endurance while they're in times of trial. I often ask God to use the challenges to grow the person's character. But for me? I want a resolution *today* and in a way that will be convenient and easy, and will result in financial blessing. Of course, I know God cares more about my character than my comfort, and that we often learn better life lessons and become more Christlike through trials than through blessings. But when I'm pouring out my heart to God, I'm not usually begging for more trials to help me be more like Christ. I want an answer, and I beg for it to come *now*.

. . . .

We often learn better life lessons and become
more Christlike through trials than through blessings.

. . . .

When my husband lost his job, we were devastated. We prayed he'd quickly get a new position, but month after month we waited. God did not provide a job immediately; instead, He provided *for* us, giving us endurance and wisdom and peace that passes all understanding. My husband's severance lasted just until he got a new job that was truly "more than all we asked or imagined"—from the job to the people to the commute. Yet, during the waiting time, after a few months into my husband's search for work, I also started looking for a job. I didn't know how God was going to help me juggle work in addition to homeschooling my first and fifth graders part-time through a charter school, writing a biweekly newspaper column, and leading a Bible study. But I felt God's prompting to take a step of faith. Eventually, because of that small step, I was hired at Moms in Prayer International headquarters in 2007. And that was exactly where God wanted me at that time. As founder Fern Nichols said, I was placed there "for such a time as this." I loved being able to freshen the look of the ministry, start our adventure into social media, begin the daily emailed scripture prayers, and work to change the ministry name from Moms In Touch International to Moms in Prayer International.

Hindsight can serve as a great teacher. Though we want to always trust God in the moment, we can gain great encouragement when, as we look back, we realize God *did* know what He was doing. If God had answered my prayer for my husband to find a new job quickly, I would never have applied to work at Moms in Prayer. I started as a part-time communications specialist, and that felt hard enough with the kid juggle. Then I was offered the position to lead the communications team. Yikes! I turned it down a couple of times before I finally listened to God saying, "Trust Me."

I had to set aside all my fears about who would pick up the kids, how I would fit in homeschool time, and how I would survive back in a career position, albeit part-time at first, while juggling home and church responsibilities. Yet God always—*always*—took care of my kids. Never has He given me an opportunity and not taken care of my family. He provided in many ways: day camp availability, friends helping with carpools, grandparents and relatives pitching in. God always worked it out where my kiddos were happy and well taken care of. And in many cases I was able to work at least part-time at home. Now I enjoy encouraging other moms as God calls them to take steps of faith.

When God Says "Trust Me"

If God is calling you to do something different—change schools, start or quit a job, or jump into a new activity where you clearly hear God saying, "This is the way; walk in it" (Isaiah 30:21)—then He will take care of all the details. After all, He truly does love your family even more than you do. Pray and see God work out the details in surprising ways.

If God had answered my pleading for my husband to find a new job quickly, we wouldn't have been in such awe over how He provided for us. We wouldn't have seen Him answer very specific requests for my husband's new job. I wouldn't have been able to help Moms in Prayer at a pivotal time in the ministry's history. I wouldn't be able to encourage moms who have to go back to work for financial reasons. And I probably wouldn't be writing this book with Sally. Did God answer my prayer for my husband's job as I had wanted? Absolutely not. But He did answer it in His perfect timing and in a way that accomplished His bigger plan.

•••••••••••••••••••••••••••••

Pray and see God work out the
details in surprising ways.

•••••••••••••••••••••••••••••

Praying Scriptures for Ourselves

Over the years, I've learned to pray for myself in a different way. Yes, I still pray specific prayers, knowing they may or may not be God's will. But when I pray scriptures for myself, I'm confident God will always say yes because I'm praying Christ's heart for me. I love Psalm 77:19-20. "Your path led through the sea, your way through the mighty waters, though your footprints were not seen. You led your people like a flock by the hand of Moses and Aaron." God's footprints might not be seen as we navigate sometimes stormy waters, but He is there, leading us through, and helping us remain unshaken.

When I'm feeling overwhelmed, one of my go-to prayers is, "Lord, be my strength in my weakness." As I have often prayed for quick healing for myself—which almost never happens—I'm reminded of 2 Corinthians 12:8-10, where the apostle Paul is struggling with such a severe pain in his side that he calls it a "thorn." He wrote:

> Three times I pleaded with the Lord to take it away from me. But he said to me, "My grace is sufficient for you, for my power is made perfect in weakness." Therefore I will boast all the more gladly about my weaknesses, so that Christ's power may rest on me. That is why, for Christ's sake, I delight in weaknesses, in insults, in hardships, in persecutions, in difficulties. For when I am weak, then I am strong.

The apostle Paul prayed and asked that the pain would be removed, but God said His grace was sufficient for him, because Christ's power is made perfect in weakness. I don't know about you, but I'm always ready to give God my weaknesses so He can fill me with *His* power, which is way more power than any I could muster on my own.

I don't know about you,
but I'm *always ready*
to give God
my weaknesses
so that He can fill me with
His power.

God created you uniquely for His purpose. You have your own calling. Remember Ephesians 2:10: "For we are God's handiwork, created in Christ Jesus to do good works, which God prepared in advance for us to do." It doesn't say God's handiwork is just your husband or your children or that woman at church you admire. *You* are God's handiwork, and He created you for a specific purpose. Isn't that amazing? If you're listening to the Holy Spirit, you will hear Him guiding you to the "good work" He prepared in advance for you to do. As it says in Isaiah 30:21, the Holy Spirit will lead: "This is the way; walk in it."

You Are Empowered by God

Most of the opportunities God brings will require that you step out in faith. Remember that you can do all things through Christ, who gives you strength (Philippians 4:13). You don't have to do anything on your own. Isn't that awesome? Just take that first, trusting step "for God's gifts and his call are irrevocable" (Romans 11:29). Don't be like the Pharisees. As it says in Luke 7:30, "The Pharisees and the experts in the law rejected God's purpose for themselves." Don't reject God's purpose for your life! Pray that God will show you what He has created you to do, and He will lead you to those opportunities—if He hasn't already.

· ·

You are God's handiwork, and He created you
for a specific purpose. Isn't that amazing?

· ·

Here's a suggested prayer based on the scripture verses we just explored.

O Lord, thank You for creating me just as You wanted me to be, weaknesses and all! Thank You that my weakness allows Your power to fill me and make me stronger. Thank You for creating me to do good works You prepared ahead of time for me to do. Wow! How incredible that the God of the universe has something specific for me to do! Lord, help me not to reject Your purpose for me like the Pharisees rejected Yours for them. As Your gifts and call are irrevocable, help me to embrace them and have the courage to step out in faith each time I hear the Holy Spirit saying, "This is the way; walk in it."

Below are other powerful verses to pray for yourself. Take them slow, pray one at a time, and expand the prayer as you go. You might find it helpful to journal your scripture prayers so you can look back to see how God has answered your requests.

When You Need Transformation
Romans 12:9-13

Love must be sincere. Hate what is evil; cling to what is good. Be devoted to one another in love. Honor one another above yourselves. Never be lacking in zeal, but keep your spiritual fervor, serving the Lord. Be joyful in hope, patient in affliction, faithful in prayer. Share with the Lord's people who are in need. Practice hospitality.

Lord, help my love be sincere. May I hate evil things in this world, and help me cling to what is good. Help me to be devoted to others in love, honoring them over myself. Empower me to never be lacking in zeal and to keep my spiritual fervor while I serve You. Lord, I need Your help to be joyful in hope, patient in affliction, faithful in prayer, and to share with Your people who are in need and to practice hospitality. This is a lot, but I trust that Your power is made perfect through my weakness. Guide me each day in putting Your words into practice.

Romans 12:2

Do not conform to the pattern of this world, but be transformed by the renewing of your mind. Then you will be able to test and approve what God's will is—his good, pleasing and perfect will.

> Lord, help me in Your strength not to conform to the pattern of this world, but to be transformed by the renewing of my mind so that I will be able to test and approve what Your good, pleasing, and perfect will is.

When You Have Frustrating Days

When I was homeschooling my children, praying the following verses got me through many frustrating days, especially verse 3, "Consider him who endured such opposition from sinners, so that you will not grow weary and lose heart." Now I cling to these verses often, no matter what I might be enduring.

Hebrews 12:1-3

Therefore, since we are surrounded by such a great cloud of witnesses, let us throw off everything that hinders and the sin that so easily entangles. And let us run with perseverance the race marked out for us, fixing our eyes on Jesus, the pioneer and perfecter of faith. For the joy set before him he endured the cross, scorning its shame, and sat down at the right hand of the throne of God. Consider him who endured such opposition from sinners, so that you will not grow weary and lose heart.

> Lord, help me to throw off everything that hinders me and the sin that so easily entangles me so I can run with perseverance the race You have marked out just for me. Help me to keep my eyes fixed

on You, Jesus, the pioneer and perfecter of my faith. You endured the cross and the shame, knowing the joy of fulfilling Your promise and offering salvation to each person who accepts You into his or her life.

Lord, as You endured opposition, help me to also endure opposition, whether it be from family members and acquaintances or from society and today's cultural pressures. Only You can help me not grow weary and lose heart while I strive to run the race You have handpicked for me.

When the Endgame Seems So Far Away

The following verse is great for those enduring long-term struggles: parents of young children, parents of children with special needs, homeschool moms, students juggling difficult classes, employees with crucial deadlines, adults caring for aging parents, parents of wayward children. Parents of teens might like this verse too!

Philippians 3:14

I press on toward the goal to win the prize for which God has called me heavenward in Christ Jesus.

Lord, please help me to keep pressing on toward the goal You have set before me. Some days, persevering is hard. Help me to keep my eyes on You and what You have called me to do.

When You're Longing for the Past

Do you have trouble not dwelling on the past, be it painful or good? Or is change approaching in some area of your life and you're resistant and fearful? You'll love these verses!

Isaiah 43:18-19

Forget the former things; do not dwell on the past. See, I am doing a new thing! Now it springs up; do you not perceive it? I am making a way in the wilderness and streams in the wasteland.

Lord, help me to forget the difficult pieces of my life that plague my mind. And help me not to dwell on the past, both the times I was hurt and the moments and memories I treasure. Remind me over and over again that You are doing a new thing. Help me to embrace the change. Help me to know that through this time of uncertainty You are paving a way in areas that seem like dry land, and You are creating streams in a desolate area—as only You can do.

When You're Under Attack and Looking for Next Steps

Are you feeling under attack and unsure what to do?

2 Chronicles 20:12

We have no power to face this vast army that is attacking us. We do not know what to do, but our eyes are on you.

O Lord, I cry out to You. I feel as though I'm being attacked on all sides, and I don't know what to do. But You always know what to do, and my eyes are on You. Help me to keep focused on You and not the circumstances surrounding me.

Isaiah 26:3

You will keep in perfect peace those whose minds are steadfast, because they trust in you.

Lord, You promise that if I trust You, my mind will be steadfast and unshaken, and You will fill me with Your peace. Help me to trust You.

Help me to keep my mind focused on You so I can remain unshaken and experience Your peace.

When You Need Encouragement

As I (Sally) began to pray God's Word over my children, putting their names into His Word and watching God answer those prayers, I wanted that for my own life. I wanted to be completely humble and gentle, bearing everyone in love. I wanted to be strong and courageous. I wanted to grow in wisdom and knowledge and live a life worthy of my calling. I wanted God to bless and move in my life as He was in the lives of my children! We have not because we ask not. So I asked God to give me eyes to see this world through His eyes and to respond with His wisdom and love.

God has grown my faith through each and every petition I pray. My favorite prayer for myself is the same as Jesus' prayer, "Not my will but Your will be done." Every day I surrender my heart, my mind, my soul, and my day to Him. This prayer of surrender is a sweet time of joy and peace. Here are a few of my favorite verses of encouragement as I pray for myself.

Jeremiah 29:11

> "For I know the plans I have for you," declares the LORD,
> "plans to prosper you and not to harm you, plans to give
> you hope and a future."

Lord, You know what is ahead for me. The plans for my life are held in Your capable hands, and those plans are to give me a hope and a future. When I am discouraged, I can lean into Your care and promises. Help me look to You and to my future with an encouraged heart.

Proverbs 3:6

In all your ways submit to him, and he will make your paths straight.

God, let Your wisdom rain down on me today and every day. I give to You all of my self, actions, priorities, relationships, and decisions. You will make my path straight, and You will make known the way to go when I am unsure. I am unshaken because Your plans stand firm.

James 1:5

If any of you lacks wisdom, you should ask God, who gives generously to all without finding fault, and it will be given to you.

Lord, I come to You in need of encouragement and wisdom. I have made mistakes. I have stumbled. My hands and my heart are open, ready to receive Your gift of wisdom. Your supply is generous, and You never withhold Your wisdom from Your children. My spirit is encouraged and steadfast because I am Your daughter.

Psalm 16:8

I keep my eyes always on the LORD. With him at my right hand, I will not be shaken.

My eyes are locked in position. They are set on You. When You and Your love are my focus, great peace and assurance fill my soul. Even when surrounded by chaos, I can fix my gaze on You and remain unshaken. Lord, I am grateful for and humbled by Your love.

Are you feeling shaken? Focus on the Lord, remembering that He is with you always.

8

Turning Your Fears into Prayers

"I do believe; help me overcome my unbelief!"

MARK 9:24

What are you afraid of? Often the fear of "What if?" holds us captive, preventing us from fully living out our potential and following God's calling. Parenthood, for example, is fraught with fears, starting with the first moment we know we're going to be moms. The fear of miscarriage is often followed by childbirth fears, newborn fears, and the ever-constant toddler fear that our little miracle might accidentally crawl, climb, or run into harm's way. As they grow, the fears grow—about safety, the wrong friends, too much screen time, and so on. And then comes teenage driving. Yikes! That's the one that has me (Cyndie) using our *Unshaken* principles to ward off fear—often.

My daughter was not quite a month past her sixteenth birthday, and there we were at the DMV—me waiting on the sidewalk while she drove off with a stranger in my old SUV. The fear was welling up inside me. As anxiety typically does, it expanded and invaded my brain, so I was no longer afraid that she'd not pass but that she'd get into a crash—and die! I had to laugh at myself, at how quickly the fear grew. I took a deep breath and started to pray, using the four steps of prayer. To stay focused, I pulled out my phone and started writing out parts of the prayer in my phone's "notes" section:

> Lord, I praise You that You love Zoe more than even I do. I praise You for being a God of peace, and that You live in her, and You can fill both of us with Your peace right now. Forgive me for my anxiety and fear, and thank You so much for answering our prayer that Zoe would have a nice lady performing the test, especially after we had only seen men giving the tests. Thank You! And, Lord, help Zoe be filled with Your peace. Calm her anxiety. Help her to focus. Please give her an easy drive. And if it's Your will, could she please pass this the first time?

As I was still praying, suddenly Zoe was standing in front of me, waving her paper. She had passed! Now, all of you with teenage drivers know the fear of them driving off without you doesn't end when they receive their license. So when I'm feeling particularly nervous, I go back through and pray the four steps of prayer.

Try it the next time fear grips your heart. Praying through praise, confession, thanksgiving, and intercession takes our eyes off our current situations (and any imaginary situations we might be concocting in our minds) and puts our eyes back on the Lord so we can stand firm and unshaken.

"Be Strong and Courageous"

Over and over in the Scriptures we're told, "Do not be afraid," or "Be strong and courageous." Why? Because it's human nature to be frightened when challenges strike. But through Christ, we can stand resolute and unshaken even in the face of great danger. Human nature craves normalcy, but our Lord often has us step out of our comfort zone so we can learn to be strong in Him alone.

Think about Joshua in the Old Testament. God was asking him to lead the Israelites as Moses had done. Can you imagine what he was thinking? Moses had led the Israelites out of slavery. He was the one who communicated directly with God, receiving the Ten Commandments as well as other instructions for living a godly life. Moses was the only human to get a glimpse of God. And now God wanted Joshua to take Moses' place and lead the Israelites to the Promised Land—the very land the Israelites had refused to enter 40 years earlier. We can assume how he must have been feeling, because God tells him over and over in Joshua 1 to be courageous and not fearful. Check it out:

Joshua 1:6-9

> Be strong and courageous, because you will lead these people to inherit the land I swore to their ancestors to give them. Be strong and very courageous. Be careful to obey all the law my servant Moses gave you; do not turn from it to the right or to the left, that you may be successful wherever you go. Keep this Book of the Law always on your lips; meditate on it day and night, so that you may be careful to do everything written in it. Then you will be prosperous and successful. Have I not commanded you? Be strong and courageous. Do not be afraid; do not be discouraged, for the LORD your God will be with you wherever you go.

God spoke these words to Joshua because he needed to hear them. Like Moses, Joshua had a great calling on his life. He was not only replacing a mighty man of God, but he would lead God's chosen people to conquer the Promised Land against fierce enemies. Do you need to hear Joshua 1:9? "Be strong and courageous! Do not tremble or be dismayed, for the LORD your God is with you wherever you go" (NASB). Repeat that verse to yourself as often as you need. God was with Joshua and was faithful to His promise. Joshua fulfilled his purpose, brought glory to God, and made an impact on a nation and a land.

••••••••••••••••••••••••••••••••

Human nature craves normalcy, but our Lord
often has us step out of our comfort zone so
we can learn to be strong in Him alone.

••••••••••••••••••••••••••••••••

We have a similar calling. No, probably not to lead a whole nation into a promised land. But God has appointed each one of us to a good purpose, and we need His strength to complete it. Sometimes, taking that step of faith to teach Sunday school, invite your friend to church, ask another person to pray with you regularly, or whatever God is calling you to do, requires courage—and lots of it! But God promises He will be with you. He never asks you to take a step of faith without giving you the ability to do it in His strength. He just asks for willing vessels that allow the Holy Spirit to lead, direct, and be used by God to fulfill His good and righteous plans. We're to fulfill God's calling on our lives, to make a difference with our loved ones and in our world for Christ, bringing Him glory. Yes, it can be scary, but God is with us wherever we go.

Following are stories of women who have transformed their fears into prayers and seen God provide in surprising ways.

Leading in the Power of the Holy Spirit

I (Sally) have been clinging to Joshua 1 since I first heard God whisper the huge step of faith He was asking of me. Fern Nichols was the founder and president of Moms in Prayer International for 30 years. Under her amazing leadership, God grew the ministry from one group of moms praying for their children at one school to groups in over 140 countries. Wow! I could never fill her shoes. Yet here was God reaching out His hand and saying, "Be strong and courageous, because you will lead these people." As the board met to discuss and pray about the decision, I prayed that if this was not God's will, I would not be selected. I knew I could become president of this life-transforming ministry only if God was leading me. If He wasn't, then it would be impossible.

After the decision was made for me to fill this role, at night the Enemy filled my mind with fear and doubt—even though I had prayed and I knew women around the world had been praying for God's choice to succeed Fern. "You are going to blow it," the Enemy said. "You are going to make mistakes; this is too big for you." And on and on. For a few nights, I could not sleep. I began to read Psalm 91 before going to bed. Then when the Enemy came calling, I would respond, "Yes, I will make mistakes, but this is God's ministry, and He will always be victorious. I am only a vessel; He works through me for His glory and His good purpose." Soon the peace that was beyond all understanding guarded my heart and mind in Christ. I cannot lead this ministry in my own strength.

Every day I surrender my work to Him and bow to His leadership. Just as He led Joshua, He will lead each one of us, if only we step out in faith, trusting that God will be our strength in our weakness. Remember Philippians 1:6. "He who began a good work in you will carry it on to completion until the day of Christ Jesus."

In my new position, I have been thrilled to meet amazing women of God who are living out God's good purpose through their lives. If I had allowed the Enemy to fill me with fear, I would have missed out on an incredible journey with God, serving Him and others. I would have missed out on getting to know my God in a powerful way and witnessing His miraculous works in action.

When I was at a Moms in Prayer European Conference, my heart was inspired by the stories of women standing firm and unshaken despite living in countries where Christianity is considered merely part of the cultural history, not relevant in today's society. Yet over and over again, I met these faith-filled families living for Christ. Many of the key leaders from the 13 countries represented at the conference have made sacrifices with great joy. The Holy Spirit is truly at work in Europe.

"Yes, *I will* make mistakes, but this is *God's ministry*, and He will *always be victorious*. I am only a vessel; He works through me for *His glory* and *His good purpose*."

—Sally Burke

Kathrin Larsen is our Moms in Prayer director in Europe, overseeing the ministry in these 22 countries. Boy, does she have a servant's heart! She's a selfless, powerful leader who is abandoned for Christ, loving her Lord, her women, and her work for our ministry. We saw the effects of her leadership throughout Europe. So imagine my surprise when her husband kept thanking us for the ministry that transformed his shy, fearful wife. Shy? Fearful? We had no idea! God only requires a willing heart, and He will empower us to live out Ephesians 2:10 in His mighty strength and power.

Here are a few more stories of how God helped women turn their fears into prayers.

Becky: Fears for a Drug-Ravaged Son

Every decision for Christ is an individual one. And we don't jump into heaven as a family unit; every child must make his or her own decision to follow Christ. Becky is a woman of God whose joy in the Lord shines through her smile. She and her husband are faithful church volunteers, teaching Sunday school to children on a weekly basis. But as a parent, Becky shares her frightening story.

My son's first overdose was at age 16. We received a call from the hospital in the wee hours of the morning. We thought he was sleeping safely in his bed. Instead, he had passed out in a park from alcohol. His companions couldn't wake him, so they ran and called 911. When our son finally woke up, his reaction wasn't relief that he was okay or appreciation for those who took care of him. Instead he was angry he was in the hospital. He rationalized that if he had been left alone, he would have woken up—eventually. At that frightening moment, we knew he was in deep trouble.

A few years later, alcohol had been replaced with heroin. After he had experienced a brief jail stay, we talked our son into entering rehab. He was set to go to the rehab interview the next day and was staying in a hotel nearby so he could meet us at our house in the morning. My husband and I felt relieved but nervous that night, both keeping our son in constant prayer.

The next morning when we called him, there was no answer. My husband drove to the hotel where he was staying and saw my son's car. Fear gripped our hearts, and we knew something was wrong. The hotel manager reluctantly told my husband which room he was in, but wouldn't open the door. So my husband called the police, who knocked the door down. My heart was crushed to hear that our son, our beautiful firstborn child, was lying facedown on the bathroom floor, unconscious with his body twisted. He was transported to the hospital after an emergency injection into his chest to counteract the heroin. When the paramedics said our son would have died in the next 20 minutes if he hadn't been found, we knew it was the prompting of the Holy Spirit to check on him that saved his life. One of the policemen told us there had been five recent deaths because of a particularly strong strain of heroin being sold in our town. None of that was a surprise to God. He had prompted my husband to act quickly and had answered our prayers for our son's protection. He was still alive.

In the hospital, we were devastated to learn that our son could still die. His kidneys and liver were failing, and he had no feeling in one of his legs because of the twisted position he had been in for several hours. We prayed at his bedside. Relatives came and laid hands on him and prayed. My dear Moms in Prayer group took that entire hour of prayer to pray only for my son. I was humbled and so thankful to the Lord for giving us so much support.

During my son's hospitalization, my husband had an important appointment for work, so he called and explained what had happened and that he wouldn't be there. As only God can do, the person he talked with said he had a friend from church who had lost his son the year before to a heroin overdose. He wanted to contact his friend and put the two men in touch. The Lord sent my husband a wonderful godly friend who wanted to walk through this with him and meet our son.

He recovered slowly from the overdose and walked with a cane for a while. Despite having a few more near-death, week-long hospital stays and having been in and out of several rehabs, he's still alive. He's been clean for almost a year now, and the Lord has blessed him with a strong work ethic and a good job with a career path.

Each frightening event we experienced from our son's addiction turned our fear into stronger faith as we prayed and watched God work. And as we prayed, our faithful God gave us peace, assuring us that He was walking with us through this painful journey. Over the years, the Lord has prompted many a nurse to witness to our son—just another sweet reminder of how much God loves him and us. Although our son is not yet a believer, as long as there is breath in his body, I will be storming the gates of heaven with my husband and my Moms in Prayer sisters for my son's salvation.

Wendy Palau: Fear Is the Opposite of Faith

Wendy Palau shoulders a burden for the lost, born out of her own experience. We appreciate her sharing this heartbreaking story of disappointment and love.

I have a story crafted by God. We all do. Maybe, like me, your story has been defined by sadness, grief, a significant loss—the kind that leaves you wondering if you'll ever be the same. I was born in Kingston, Jamaica, to a family of godly, kingdom-minded people. My father, a businessman, threw himself into any evangelistic effort that came to our island. In 1993, I heard the evangelist Luis Palau was coming for a crusade and that one of his sons would be staying in our home. That Friday night, Andrew Palau walked into our kitchen. Just over a year later, we were married. I was transported from island life to rainy but beautiful Portland, Oregon. The first few years of our marriage were good ones. We worked with the Palau team, traveling the country as Andrew directed evangelistic festivals. We were in a groove, and felt God's hand on our family. Three years after our wedding, we had our first son, Chris. Fifteen months later, our second son, Jonathan, arrived. Amazing, healthy, and beautiful boys.

We had just moved to Fort Lauderdale, Florida, when I became pregnant with our third. The first trimester was horrid. Sick. Tired. Hungry. Not hungry. It was exactly what I'd experienced with my first two. Andrew and I followed the doctor's orders to the letter: regular check-ups, prenatal vitamins. Whatever he said, we did.

Then one horrifying day the doctor couldn't find a heartbeat. The ultrasound showed our beautiful, tiny baby, yet his heartbeat was gone. We were devastated.

A year later I became pregnant once again. Many women have miscarriages yet go on to have healthy pregnancies. All should be fine, I was told. We breathed a bit lighter after the 12-week mark. Yet three weeks later, our little baby was gone. Another tiny, precious baby. Another life we had dreamed about loving—gone.

Twelve months later, I was pregnant again. Fear was a constant, nagging companion. I longed for this baby, but I couldn't imagine going through the sadness again. I determined to pray my way through the pregnancy and asked many to join me. This baby would survive, and I would do *anything* in my power to ensure it.

At 20 weeks, the doctor couldn't find a heartbeat. I still remember leaving the hospital with heavy, empty arms. It seemed so wrong. I laid down in bed that night and wasn't sure how to wake the next morning. I wanted to sleep forever; it was the only time the darkness went away.

I felt guilty about how much I flirted with anger toward God. He could have saved my babies—all three of them. I believed in His power to save them. Yet when I asked He said no. I called Him Lord, the same word Martha used in John 11:3. It means Master, a person exercising absolute ownership rights. I called Him Lord *all* the time. Whenever I asked Him for protection, provision, strength, health, peace—every time I talked to Him. Was He really my Lord in the middle of this agony?

Still, I kept opening my Bible. I found comfort there. Everything I found told me He is good, that He works things together for good, that He has good plans, that His character is good. Did I really believe this? I kept asking, "Lord, I believe. Please help my unbelief." I turned my eyes toward Him. He comforted me.

Slowly, God began to reveal His heart toward adoption. I was certain I couldn't do it. I could not love a non-biological child the way we loved our boys. Where would that love come from? I was scared to death. A child born from another woman's womb who was meant to be in our family? It made no sense to me.

....

I kept asking, "Lord, I believe. Please help
my unbelief." I turned my eyes toward
Him. He comforted me. —Wendy Palau

....

A conversation I had with my mother changed things. I was telling her about all my fears. She said, "Wendy, if you and Andrew don't adopt because of fear, you'll regret it all your lives. Fear is the opposite of faith." I knew she was right. Within 18 months, and with meager, mustard-seed faith, we were flying to Addis Ababa, Ethiopia, to meet our baby girl.

What I didn't realize or see in the middle of my sadness was that there was an abandoned child on the other side of the world who had her own story. She had been delivered to an orphanage on the tenth day of her life. They had named her Rediet, which means "help of God." This baby, left abandoned, was our "help of God." She needed us. We needed her. Her tiny little self was God's beautiful blessing and goodness being poured into our lives. And we've experienced it every day. And the love I was so afraid wouldn't be there? Oh, how we love our girl!

God is good, and I've tasted it. I feared it wasn't so, when my heart was broken and grieving. But as I barely held on, I tasted His goodness in ways I never could have imagined or planned. He's working out beautiful things for you, too, just as He did for me. It's worth it. It's worth that meager faith. It's worth those nights calling out to Him for help. He's the God who raises the poor from the dust and the needy from the ash heap. He did it for me. He did it for my daughter. And He will do it for you.

Jennifer Kennedy Dean: Fear, Faith, and Finances

Jennifer Kennedy Dean is the executive director of the Praying Life Foundation. As an author and speaker, she has made an impact on generations through her books, encouraging us to live a praying life.

I had written two books. My children were young, and my husband, Wayne, worked for a large corporation. We had a comfortable life. We had experienced a long period of unemployment, but that was in the past now. Opportunities to speak and minister were increasing, and I had to pass up many invitations because it just wasn't feasible with my family commitments. One evening, as we were discussing some speaking invitations and whether or not I should accept, Wayne broached a subject that would change almost everything about our lives. What if he quit his full-time job and became my full-time manager, and was present for our sons when I traveled?

I liked everything about that except the no-regular-paycheck part. I had lived through a stretch of unemployment, and now everything was on an even keel. I liked status quo. I asked God to let Wayne know what a bad idea this was. I asked God to let me keep my life as it was. But Wayne felt called. Not just inclined, but called. So with great trepidation I agreed.

Because of that decision, I could commit to more speaking engagements and writing opportunities. Wayne and I had years of working side by side, both our offices in our home, committed to the same vision. It deepened our marriage and our enjoyment of each other. Even the financial challenges gave us the opportunity to grow together in our faith and commitment to following our mutual call. Our three sons had their dad's presence and attention full-time. Wayne never missed a sports practice, let alone a game. He was there for them for every detail of their lives.

We didn't know back then that we would lose him so early. When my sons were in their twenties, Wayne passed away of brain cancer. Because of his decision to quit his job—the one I so earnestly prayed against—my sons had more of their father than many whose fathers live well into old age. Because of that decision, the 26 years we had together were rich and sweet. Because of that decision, everything about the ministry has Wayne's fingerprints on it.

I've learned that risky is safe when it's in response to God's call. Because God is fully committed to seeing me joyful and fulfilled in Him, not looking for that contentment in my circumstances, He will bring me into places where I am compelled to depend on Him and learn by experience how faithful He is. When my lips were saying, "Lord, please change Wayne's mind," He heard my heart saying, "I want what You want." As it turns out, God is not a lip reader so much as He is a heart reader.

●●●●●●●●●●●●●●●●●●●●●●●●●●●●●●

I've learned that risky is safe when it is in
response to God's call. Because God is
fully committed to seeing me joyful and fulfilled in Him. —Jennifer Kennedy Dean

●●●●●●●●●●●●●●●●●●●●●●●●●●●●●●

9

Waiting on God's Perfect Timing

Wait for the LORD; be strong and take
heart and wait for the LORD.

PSALM 27:14

Waiting. Who likes to wait? We live an instantaneous society. You can pop a frozen meal in the microwave, and in a few minutes—ta-da! Hot and ready for devouring. Or even easier, drive through a fast-food lane. Want to know the fastest route to a location? Just ask Siri! Who would go the route that's seven minutes longer if their phone or car's GPS can give them a shorter route?

Yet God's timing is rarely on our timetable. He's not rushed, but His timing is always perfect. Always! Oh, but how hard it is to wait. Remember Abram and Sarai in Genesis 16? God promised Abram an heir with so many offspring he couldn't even count them. Yet Abram was in his eighties with no children. Would you start doubting right about then? So did his wife, Sarai! Being a wife who took matters into her own hands, she had this idea as shared in Genesis 16:2: "The LORD has kept me from having children. Go, sleep with my slave; perhaps I can build a family through her."

Did Abram object? Nope. Verse 2 also says, "Abram agreed to what Sarai said."

Now check out verse 4. "He slept with Hagar, and she conceived. When she knew she was pregnant, she began to despise her mistress." Yeah, so the take-matters-into-your-own-hands backfired big time. Not only were Sarai/Sarah and her servant Hagar now at odds with one another, but Hagar became pregnant with Ishmael, the father of the Muslim faith.

In chapter 17, over a decade later, God tells a 99-year-old Abram, "I will bless her [Sarah] and will surely give you a son by her. I will bless her so that she will be the mother of nations; kings of peoples will come from her" (verse 16). And what did Abram/Abraham do? "Abraham fell facedown; he laughed and said to himself, 'Will a son be born to a man a hundred years old? Will Sarah bear a child at the age of ninety?'" (verse 17).

The answer was yes!

Waiting is hard. "But do not forget this one thing, dear friends: With the Lord a day is like a thousand years, and a thousand years are like a day. The Lord is not slow in keeping his promise, as some understand slowness. Instead he is patient with you, not wanting anyone to perish, but everyone to come to repentance" (2 Peter 3:8-10).

Waiting on God's Plan

Frequently, God has a plan different from the one we anticipated. In my (Cyndie's) Bible, Psalm 27:14 has notes scrawled around it with dates I claimed the prayer, *Lord, help me be strong and take heart and wait for the Lord.* One of the dates was during college acceptance season for my son. We waited and waited and waited, and the college Elliott really wanted to attend eventually said no. What devastation! We thought for sure that's where God wanted him, and that He was going to surprise and delight us with the scholarships and funds to pay for the outrageously expensive tuition.

Shortly after we found out Elliott didn't get in, my niece messaged, saying her alma mater had a great new arts department—including film, my son's passion. As I looked at the cost of tuition, I couldn't believe it: half the cost of his dream college, and it was a Christian school. I went to my son's room to see what he thought and was surprised to hear him say, "Okay." As we climbed aboard the plane after a quick two-day, one-night stay to see the college, I asked him again what he thought. He had reservations—mostly because it wasn't his dream college—but said, "God already told me that's where I'm supposed to go." During the waiting time, God had prepared Elliott's heart for the college He had planned for him to attend.

Prolonged waiting periods can make our hearts feel shaken. But cling to who God is: faithful, trustworthy, loving, sovereign, purposeful. Trust that God's at the helm and that His timing is always perfect. As Psalm 130:5 says, "I wait for the LORD, my whole being waits, and in his word I put my hope."

....

Prolonged waiting periods can make our hearts
feel shaken. But cling to who God is: faithful, trustworthy, loving, sovereign, purposeful.

....

Here are two more stories of waiting on the Lord and His timing.

Jill Savage: Waiting on God's Provision

Isn't it awesome when our kids catch the vision to pray and listen for God's answer? We love this testimony from Jill Savage, the founder and director of Hearts at Home, as God used a time of waiting in her daughter's life.

Anne, I need to talk with you." I began the dreaded conversation with our almost 16-year-old daughter one Saturday morning. "You know Dad and I were saving money to buy a

third car for the family so when you turned 16 you'd have a vehicle to use. What we didn't count on was our well running dry
(oh, the joys of country living!). When we had to have a new
well dug, we had to use the car money. Now we won't be able to
purchase a car."

Anne's face reflected her disappointment. I was disappointed
too. With four children at the time, I was looking forward to
some help with the taxi responsibilities. "I'm bummed, Mom,
but I understand. I guess I'll just have to pray for a car."

I affirmed her decision, but I had no idea how serious she
was. Several weeks after our conversation Anne popped into the
kitchen while I was making dinner and said, "Mom, you know
how I told you I would pray for a car? I just wanted you to know
I'm praying specifically like you've taught me. I'm praying that
it would have an automatic transmission because I don't know
how to drive a stick shift. I'm also praying that it would be a
four-door vehicle since I'll be taking my siblings so many places,
and it's a pain to climb in and out of the backseat of a two-door.
And I decided to ask God if it would be possible for it to be blue,
because that's my favorite color."

I stared at her in astonishment. "Wow! That's a tall order," I
responded. "I think if a car becomes available, you'd better be
ready to take it as it is, even if it means learning to drive a stick,
climbing out of the backseat, or learning to like another color."

"I know, Mom," she replied, "but God tells us to ask specifically, so I am. And I believe He can provide if it's in His will."

I was astonished at my daughter's spiritual maturity, but my
heart was torn in two directions. I was so proud of Anne's faith—
she was taking God at His word, and her belief was strong. At
the same time I desperately wanted to protect my girl from disappointment. This *was* a tall order, and even though I believed
God *could* provide, I just didn't know that He really *would*, and
I didn't want her to get hurt.

Several days after that conversation, I stumbled out of bed and decided to check email before everyone woke up and the morning chaos began. I noticed an email from a man at our church who never emailed us. His name was Mike. When I opened the email and began to read, tears started rolling down my cheeks:

> Hello, Mark and Jill,
>
> I'm in the process of purchasing a new car and my old one still runs fine, but it isn't worth a whole lot. I've been praying about what to do with the old car, and today, as I was walking down the hall at work, I thought of you. I think you have a daughter who will be driving soon, and I'm wondering if you would like a car for her. Here are the basic details: it's a 1983 Honda Accord, automatic transmission, four doors. Don't know that it matters, but it's blue. Let me know if you'd be interested. If you are, I'm willing to give it to your family.

I couldn't believe my eyes. I was humbled by my daughter's faith and God's miraculous provision. "Yes, Mike," I whispered out loud, "it does matter that it's blue. It matters a lot!"

Cyndie: Waiting on a Loved One's Salvation

For those who are praying for the long haul, who are trying to remain unshaken while praying for the salvation of a child or spouse or other loved one, let me (Cyndie) encourage you with my own story about my brother—the result of persevering in prayer.

I am the fourth of six children born to a lifelong Marine. The full hoo-rah, and all. Now, my dad, who was close to his brothers and brothers-in-arms, was blessed with a baby girl. Then another girl. And another. And another. And another. Five in total. They had assumed the last bouncy baby would be a girl too. But much to everyone's surprise, the sixth baby was wrapped in a blue blanket. Yep, my Marine dad finally had a *boy*! I was four years old when my cute little brother was born, and I vividly remember going with the excited neighbors to pick out something blue before stopping by the base hospital to meet Cliff John Claypool.

As you can imagine, there were high hopes for this only boy. But once he started school those hopes were challenged, one by one. My parents were told their little boy had a genius-level IQ but also had such a severe learning disability that he would never be able to read. My dad didn't take that answer as final. He tried and tried to teach Cliff to read. Picture this, a retired Marine Gunnery Sergeant who made people jump at his first command, sitting at a dining room table with a defiant child who typically did the opposite of whatever was asked. They're trying to work on decoding two-dimensional, written words—the very thing that was the hardest for my brother. Needless to say, not a lot of academic progress was made.

What my brother did learn in school was that he was a good fighter. By junior high, he had aligned himself with the other good fighters: our local gang. Before he was even an adult, he had dropped out of high school, married the mother of his child, and made a name for himself among the homeboys and, well, with the police. To say that I prayed for my brother a lot would be an understatement.

When he was sentenced to prison, I begged God for his release. But God had a better plan.

My mom and I would often go down to the prison, taking his two daughters to visit their dad. But then my brother— who continued to be seen as a prizefighter for the gang, even in prison—was moved to a penitentiary hours and hours away. I was devastated.

I prayed that he would be able to stay local so we could visit, so his girls could know him. But God had a different plan.

My heart's cry was that my brother would become a Christian sold out for Christ, that he'd have a transformed life and walk closely with his Savior. Despite a pastor telling me the statistics showing the likelihood of Cliff having a genuine conversion in prison were low, I persevered in persistent prayer, pouring out my aching heart to God.

Each time we finally figured out how we'd go visit him at his new prison, he would get moved to another location. It was agonizing. I imagined my brother lonely and devastated, which broke my heart. Yet God knew he needed to be isolated—and not just from family. He was thrown in the "hole" (solitary confinement) for instigating a fight that didn't stop until the security guard had shot my brother in the shoulder. In pain and alone and with only a Bible as his companion, Cliff finally surrendered his pride to God.

As he prayed, he asked God to open his eyes so he could read His Word. And God did!

My brother said it was like scales falling off his eyes, and the Word of God leapt off the page for the first time for him. Later, he tried yet again to pass the high school equivalency exam, the GED. Each time he'd taken the test previously, he completely failed because he couldn't understand the questions he was reading. This time, however, he passed, scoring 99 percent in comprehension. That was nothing short of a miracle!

I still remember Cliff's collect call from the prison. Usually when he called, he'd be sad about his divorce or missing his girls. But this call was different. I was talking to a transformed man of God! Our heavenly Father had heard and answered the thousands of prayers my family had cried out for my brother. And, as always, God's timing was perfect. We wanted immediate answers, but God had the endgame in mind.

Now my brother is married to a wonderful navy nurse and has another adorable, spunky daughter. After barely passing any classes in school, he went on to graduate from college—and *seminary*! Yep, my little brother is now a pastor at a small church, ministering to those in the very same area where he once made a name for himself as a gangbanger.

God is making a name for Himself through Cliff's transformed life. Seeing my brother lead whole families to Christ and baptize them in the very church where we once attended and where countless prayers were prayed on his behalf brings tears to my eyes. God truly does transform lives and answer prayers—in His perfect timing.

∙∙∙∙∙∙∙∙∙∙∙∙∙∙∙∙∙∙∙∙∙∙∙∙∙∙∙∙∙∙∙

We wanted immediate answers, but
God had the endgame in mind.

∙∙∙∙∙∙∙∙∙∙∙∙∙∙∙∙∙∙∙∙∙∙∙∙∙∙∙∙∙∙∙

If my parents had their way, God would have answered their prayers for their son back when he was in grade school. But God had a bigger purpose, a purpose that involved making an impact on an entire community for Christ. That was worth the wait.

Are You Waiting?

As you read this beautiful psalm, think about a time when you waited for God to save you. Or maybe you're experiencing that now.

> I waited patiently for the LORD; he turned to me and heard my cry. He lifted me out of the slimy pit, out of

the mud and mire; he set my feet on a rock and gave me a firm place to stand. He put a new song in my mouth, a hymn of praise to our God. Many will see and fear the LORD and put their trust in him. Blessed is the one who trusts in the LORD, who does not look to the proud, to those who turn aside to false gods. Many, LORD my God, are the wonders you have done, the things you planned for us. None can compare with you; were I to speak and tell of your deeds, they would be too many to declare (Psalm 40:1-5).

Our prayer for you is that you will learn to stand unshaken, no matter what happens along your path and no matter how long you must wait. Keep praying. Keep focusing on the truths of Christ. Keep going to God in confession to maintain a heart after God. Keep remembering the prayers God has answered. Keep being thankful. Keep praying through the Scriptures. While waiting can be agonizing, look to the One who has a purposeful plan for your life and for the life of your loved ones. If God has you waiting, it's because He has a bigger and better purpose, far greater than you can imagine. "Yet the LORD longs to be gracious to you; therefore he will rise up to show you compassion. For the LORD is a God of justice. Blessed are all who wait for him!" (Isaiah 30:18).

If *God* has you *waiting,*
it's because He has a
bigger and *better purpose,*
far *greater* than you
can imagine.

Part 4

Stories of Unshaken Inspiration

10

Unleashing God's Power to Do More Than We Can Imagine

Now to him who is able to do immeasurably more than all
we ask or imagine, according to his power that is at work
within us, to him be glory in the church and in Christ
Jesus throughout all generations, for ever and ever! Amen.

EPHESIANS 3:20-21

*E*phesians 3:20-21 is a stunning passage! God doesn't just answer our prayers; He can answer them in ways that are so over the top—so beyond what we ask or imagine—that we can't even measure them! And this portion of Scripture reminds us that God's strength and power are at work within us. Why? So Christ Jesus can be glorified throughout the church for every generation, forever and ever. Wow!

What is on your heart? What's that deep ache that, every time it comes to mind, your stomach feels a little kick or your heart feels a little pinch? Sometimes we spend so much time worrying about problems that we forget to pray about them. We stew and complain and whine about our predicaments, but forget to ask the One in control of the entire universe. Have you poured out your heart to our Almighty Father? Psalm 5:3 says, "In the morning, LORD, you hear my voice; in the morning I lay my requests before you and wait expectantly." Are you waiting expectantly for God to answer?

Experiencing God's Orchestration

When I (Cyndie) was pregnant with my first child, I had no idea what we were going to do for childcare. We couldn't afford to go without my income, yet we couldn't afford all-day childcare. And we (rightly) suspected that once our child was born, we were going to want to see him more than just evenings and weekends. So we prayed. And prayed. And prayed some more. Yet each avenue we explored was a closed door. Nothing was right. I was vacillating between faith in a big God and, well, pregnancy freak-out.

••••••••••••••••••••••••••••••

Sometimes we spend so much time worrying about
problems that we forget to pray about them.

••••••••••••••••••••••••••••••

Then a few months before my son was born the newspaper where I was an editor bought the paper just three miles from my house. After much prayer, what was an overwhelming situation turned into a more-than-all-I-asked-or-imagined answer to prayer. By the grace of God, I was given one of two coveted feature-writer positions at the newly combined newspaper. Besides being my heart's desire, it was a flexible position that allowed me to work some from home, which I could almost never do as an editor and page designer. Plus I was moved to the office just seven minutes from my home, and I could get there without any freeway driving! On top of that, a couple from church, longtime friends, offered to watch my son. Our boys grew up together as little buddies.

The added blessing was that my husband went to work early and usually got home about 3:00 p.m. I worked from home in the morning during my son's nap, dropped him off at my friends' about 1:00 p.m., and then worked the later shift in the office. My little boy was only at his friend's house two or three hours a day, and to him it was just a fun playdate with his best friend. Even now, 20 years later, I can't believe how God orchestrated the pieces to make all that work so smoothly. It was truly more than all I asked or imagined!

Experiencing a Ripe Harvest

I (Sally) remember watching my daughter Aubrie experience God answering prayers for her classmates in ways that were far more than we had asked or imagined. During her senior year in high school, my Moms in Prayer group prayed that the senior class would make an impact on their campus for Christ, leaving a legacy that would bring glory to God and bless their school. Little did we know how God would answer those prayers. A few of us had senior girls who decided to start a coeducational Bible study. They yearned for their friends to grow in their relationship with the Lord and become passionate about Jesus Christ. The Bible study group grew, and several of its members decided to pray on Friday mornings for their fellow students to know Jesus.

I remember when my daughter and her friend shared with me what had occurred during her Christian school's week in the mountains. Their eyes were filled with wonder. Ninety-one of their fellow students had heard the gospel from a speaker and responded by falling on their faces and repenting of their sins. Students received Jesus for the first time, and some rededicated their lives to the Lord. As Aubrie stood among them in awe of what she was witnessing, her principal came up to her and acknowledged this great awakening had occurred through prayer.

Many of these new believers started to attend the student-led Bible study. I asked my daughter what they were teaching. She said they were going through the book of Romans line by line. Soon several more students at the campus received Jesus. They witnessed an

Acts-type revival! God answered our prayers immeasurably more than we could have asked or imagined.

Fern Nichols's Big and Bold Prayers for the Ministry

One of our favorite stories of God working above and beyond what we can imagine is how Moms in Prayer International exploded throughout America in 1988. Here's how founder Fern Nichols explains it:

God kept increasing my vision. At first it was prayer for my children and the school they attended where we lived in Canada, and then the vision increased for all the schools in that area to be covered. Then in 1985 God moved our family from British Columbia, Canada, to Poway near San Diego, California. I knew no one. One simple prayer emerged: "Lord, I need one other mom to pray with me." By the end of the school year, 15 moms were coming to my home to pray for the high school.

In 1988 we had our first Moms In Touch (now called Moms in Prayer) retreat. Thirty-five women were at a retreat center together in a fireside room, thanking God for all the answers to prayer we had seen since praying in a Moms In Touch group. The Holy Spirit was moving sweetly among us. A prayer emerged through united hearts, and we cried out, "Lord, we have been changed, our children and the school have been changed, and we now ask that all the schools in the San Diego area be covered in prayer."

Soon the prayer grew even bigger. We prayed for every California school to have a Moms In Touch group. Then our faith grew to ask for the whole Northwest. The Holy Spirit moved our prayers across the United States and then around the world. There was silence, then one mom prayed, "Lord, who can tell the women of the world about Moms In Touch?" There was a pause.

"Dobson, that's who. Lord, we ask to be on his program." I think we were all stunned at first by the request, and then there was a joyous agreement.

Three months later, without anyone contacting Focus on the Family, LuAnne Crane from Focus called me, asking about the ministry. She caught the vision but said she couldn't promise anything since a lot of requests crossed Dr. Dobson's desk. Did we ever pray! We were so bold that not only did we ask to be on the program, but that God would give us two days just in case a mom didn't hear the first day. God answered above and beyond our request. He gave us three days! Twelve other moms joined Dr. Dobson and me in the studio. God knew this message of hope needed to be heard by moms. The result of the program was over 24,000 responses. Needless to say, the Moms in Prayer ministry has never been the same since that day. We're now in every state in America and in more than 140 countries!

We hope by sharing the following prayer stories that you, too, will be encouraged to pray big, bold prayers and let God answer them in ways that are over-the-top more than you ever anticipated. Enjoy these additional stories.

Be encouraged to pray
big, bold prayers
and *let God answer* them
in ways that are *over-the-top*
more than you ever anticipated.

Here are two more stories that illustrate God's incredible answers to prayer.

Jill Savage: Got Bread? Got Milk?

Jill Savage, the founder of Hearts at Home, shared this story of God going above and beyond.

After working for some time at a new nonprofit ministry, my husband's boss came to him with a dilemma. "Mark, we've temporarily lost the private funding we've had for your salary. The donor's investments are tied up and they need a few months to recover. We believe we'll be able to reinstate your salary in three months with back pay, but until then we can't pay you. If you need to seek out another job, we understand. But if you can stick with us, we'd love to have you stay on."

That was quite a request to make of a man with a large family to feed. Mark came home and we talked about the situation. We agreed to pray about it individually for several days before making a decision. Later we discovered that both of us were hearing two words: *Trust Me.* We felt we weren't to make a change, and that Mark was to continue working at his job without pay. It was a scary thought, yet we both had an unusual peace about it (and no, we didn't have three months' worth of salary in the bank like you're supposed to have!).

I immediately got busy doing what I could. I called our utility companies and creditors and made whatever arrangements were possible for delayed or smaller payments for a limited time. I looked at what little money we had in our savings and divided it up to pay the bills we would need to pay. I then took an inventory of the food in our pantry and two freezers, writing down everything we had in the house to eat, including the two cans of beets pushed to the back of the pantry shelf I didn't know we had. I sat down and laid out a possible meal plan for 12 weeks.

When Mark came home from work that afternoon, I shared the results of my planning with him. "I've made arrangements for the monthly bills, and I've figured out a way we can eat without having to go to the grocery store. The only things we won't have are the fresh foods like bread and milk, but we can pray specifically for those."

Honestly, in my mind, I thought that maybe God would send a music opportunity my way—sometimes I'd sing or play for weddings and earn $50 or so. Mark also installed carpet on the side, and I thought maybe God would send him a small carpet job each month that would pay enough for us to go to the grocery store to get bread, milk, and maybe fresh fruits and vegetables.

We shared with our children that we were in a season of trusting. No new clothes, no convenience snack food in the snack drawer, no extra money to go out for ice cream. We reassured them that we would be okay, but that we all had to respect the sacrifices and be thankful for what we had. Every meal we sat around the table holding hands to pray, thanking God for how He had already provided and making our simple request for bread and milk.

A couple of weeks after we started our faith journey, I received a call from my neighbor Orville. We live in the country, so our neighbors aren't the "over the fence" type of neighbors. Rather, they live "down the road," and we don't often interact with one another. Orville farmed all the land around our home, so he'd stop by and chat during planting and harvest season, but other than that we didn't see one another very often.

When I picked up the phone, Orville said, "Jill, do you need some bread?"

I was caught off guard by the absence of small talk you often have at the start of a phone conversation and by the nature of his question. "Well, Orville, actually, yes, we do need some bread," I responded almost with a question in my voice.

"Okay, I'll be by in a few minutes," he continued. "I've got some you can have." I hung up the phone thinking that was the oddest phone conversation I'd ever had. *Trust Me,* I heard once again.

Within minutes Orville's truck pulled into our driveway. As I walked out to meet him I noticed the bed of his truck was piled high...with bread! As Orville parked and got out of the truck, I teasingly said, "Orville, what did you do? Did you rob a bread store?"

"Oh, no," he responded. "I have an agreement with a couple of grocery stores to haul away their expired bread products. I take it out of its wrappings and feed it to my cows. Honestly, there's always more than I can use. Much of it is still good, so Betty and I always pull some out for ourselves before I head out to the barn. Today as I was driving home, I suddenly thought, *Those Savages have a lot of kids. Maybe they'd like some of this bread.* So I called you."

I stood there amazed with tears in my eyes. When I was finally able to pull myself together to get a few words out, I said, "Orville, are you aware of what's going on with our family?" Looking puzzled, he replied that he didn't know what I was talking about. I briefly filled him in on Mark's situation with not being paid at work, and I finished with, "So every evening when we sit down together as a family, we thank God for what He's provided, and we pray for bread and milk."

Orville's eyes lit up, "You need milk?" he asked. Before I could respond he opened the cab of his truck to reveal about 12 gallons of milk.

"These expired yesterday, but if you freeze them, they'll be just fine," he declared. I couldn't hold it together anymore. I stood there looking at that bread and milk that had been delivered in the most unlikely way, and I thanked God in my heart for being trustworthy.

Orville offered to carry the milk into my kitchen while I dug through the bed of his truck to find whatever bread I wanted. As I began to look, I was amazed at the selection: English muffins, donuts, bagels, wheat bread, white bread, raisin bread, and rainbow bread (I didn't even know rainbow bread existed). Most of these were name brand, what I would consider expensive, breads that we'd never eaten before. I filled several grocery sacks with the bread I knew our family would eat. Orville helped me carry it all into the house. After placing all the milk jugs in our chest freezer, I gave Orville a big hug. I thanked him for his gift and said, "Orville, you didn't just think that the Savage family might need this food, you listened and responded to God's still small voice. Thank you for listening."

I was home alone when Orville came that day. You can imagine the surprise Mark and the kids experienced when they arrived home and I was able to tell them what God did. As we gathered around the table that evening, we held hands, thanked God for His incredible provisions, and didn't ask for a single thing!

Retta Berry: A New, Surprising, Life-Changing Diagnosis

The story below from Retta Berry is beyond anything our human brains could ever have imagined. And through the miracle God performed in Retta's family, others are being healed physically and spiritually, with many coming to Christ. God has given her a public platform to share her testimony to the media, to Congress, and even to the president of the United States.

My husband, Joe, and I have three amazing children. Our oldest son, Zach, is 22 and is an incredible son, big brother, and our first miracle. God also blessed us with Noah and Alexis, twins, who are 19. We have three miracles who are alive today, and we thank God for each one, knowing His plans are so much better than ours. "Now to him who is able to do immeasurably more than all we ask or imagine, according to his power that is at work within us, to him be glory in the church and in Christ Jesus throughout all generations, for ever and ever! Amen!" (Ephesians 3:20-21).

Noah and Alexis were born with a lot of medical problems. They were colicky for 15 months, cried nonstop throughout the day and night, had seizures, had urine reflux up into their kidneys, threw up daily, and never reached their developmental milestones on time. When they were nine months old, we were quickly thrown into a new world, one filled with medical specialists, therapists, hospital visits, testing, and emergency rooms. Our world was turned upside down in the blink of an eye. We prayed God would lead us to answers and healing. We prayed for a miracle.

When Noah and Alexis were close to two years of age, they were both diagnosed with cerebral palsy, based on evidence found on MRIs. We had been praying for answers, so we thanked God that we finally had one. We moved forward with the diagnosis and continued Noah's and Alexis's physical, speech, occupational, and early intervention therapies, as well as their ongoing medical treatments. I continued my daily research, which the Lord had led me to when they were nine months old, in hopes of finding help for their many challenges. We continued to pray for a miracle, knowing that with God all things are possible.

I was attending Bible Study Fellowship in 2002 when I received a call from my group leader. She told me the Lord laid me on her heart to go into a leadership position in BSF. I was puzzled. BSF is very structured and has strict attendance rules. I struggled to make it every week because of Noah's and Alexis's health issues. She explained how that concerned her at first, but God continued to lay me on her heart, through prayer. I was asked to pray for three days and seek God's will for this position. I agreed and prayed for three days, not knowing how I could possibly handle more responsibility with Noah's and Alexis's needs. I chose not to lean on my own understanding, and instead trusted God to show me His will. He answered my prayers.

On the third day of praying, the Lord said no to BSF and led me back into researching for my children. I had been doing research for four years, though I had recently put down all my research materials because Alexis needed full-time care. At the time, we had started looking at wheelchairs and feeding tubes for her, and we never thought she would live independently. The very day God spoke to me, He led me directly to a file of hundreds of articles I had put in my desk drawer. The Holy Spirit led me through article after article, until He showed me the one titled "Deft Diagnosis: Segawa's Dystonia Mimics Cerebral Palsy but Is Treatable with a Medication." As I read the article, I knew without a doubt that Alexis fit the diagnosis. God was leading us, through prayer, each step of the way.

Through a series of miraculous events, we were at the University of Michigan, in Dr. John Fink's office, on April 10, 2002. We started Alexis on the drug L-DOPA, and she went from a life of wheelchairs and feeding tubes to walking, talking, dancing, gymnastics, soccer, and every sport we never dreamed possible for her. Noah's onset of dystonia started a few months later. We placed Noah on L-DOPA, through God's leading and against medical advice, and his response defied medical understanding. God was moving mountains!

The Lord led me to start a website in 2003, and He used it to help people around the world who were misdiagnosed. Every time we had opportunities to do a media piece to share God's story in our lives, I would ask a large group of people to pray. We prayed that whomever God wanted to reach, they would find themselves tuning into the channel or picking up the magazine article. Over the years, I have received calls from people around the world whose lives were changed after finding Noah's and Alexis's story in surprising ways. One person shared how there was only one channel that worked on their television, and it was the one airing this story. People picked up magazines they had never read before and opened right to the account of God moving in our lives. God reached quadriplegics who, after hearing about the transformation Noah and Alexis experienced, were soon playing tennis and running races. Our God is alive and active, and He hears our prayers!

In 2008 the Lord brought us to San Diego to merge my passion of helping others with Joe's job. Joe went to work for a company making equipment that would be able to diagnose kids like Noah and Alexis at birth. Little did we know God drew us here for a purpose that would be beyond anything we could have possibly envisioned. A year after moving to San Diego, Alexis started struggling for breath. We almost lost her on many occasions as paramedics came rushing into our home, trying to get her breathing. After 18 months of searching for answers, the very equipment God used to bring us to San Diego to help others saved Alexis's life. Our God is a miracle worker!

God has blessed us with opportunities to share His story through hundreds of media outlets around the world. He has placed me, a praying mom, in front of thousands of brilliant scientists, researchers, Congress, and even the president of the United States to share His story in our lives. He has worked through each of these opportunities to reach millions of people who need answers, hope, and Jesus. We have witnessed people being drawn to Jesus as we share and pray with them. God has done more than anything we could have ever dreamed or imagined possible. He's a God of miracles, He hears our prayers, and His plans are so much better than ours!

No matter what you're struggling with, God has a plan that's truly more than all you ask or imagine. Hang in there! Meditate on Psalm 16:8. "I keep my eyes always on the Lord. With him at my right hand, I will not be shaken."

11

Embracing God's Peace and Living Unshaken

One thing I do: forgetting what lies behind and straining
forward to what lies ahead, I press on toward the goal
for the prize of the upward call of God in Christ Jesus.

PHILIPPIANS 3:13-14 (ESV)

*I*t's one thing to read a book about standing firm and becoming unshaken despite the storms in our lives. It's completely different to take these principles to heart to become transformed by God, shunning fear and embracing His strength, wisdom, and power. In this chapter we want to each take a section to encourage you as you apply these truths to your daily walk with the Lord.

A Final Word from Cyndie

The ups and downs of life can be hard. When I think about everything my family and extended family have endured because of wacky and extreme health issues, financial troubles, and the consequences of poor choices, it's somewhat shocking to realize we keep smiling. Why do we? Because we can trust that a loving God is working things out for a good purpose and that He's transforming each one of us for something larger than ourselves.

You might have guessed that one of my favorite verses is Ephesians 2:10, which we have visited several times during this journey.

This awe-inspiring verse is worth memorizing and repeating daily. "For we are God's handiwork, created in Christ Jesus to do good works, which God prepared in advance for us to do."

Wow! The God of creation loves me so much that He wants the very best for me, and He handpicked "good works" for me to do that He prepared in advance for me. He doesn't give us what we want just because we're begging and pleading for it; God answers prayers in His perfect timing and in ways that will surprise and delight us so we'll know beyond a shadow of a doubt that He was the one who answered those prayers.

Years ago, while sitting in my quiet-time chair, it finally hit me—a truth you've already heard in this book: God cares more about our character than our comfort.

One of my nephews has suffered from an extreme seizure disorder since he was a small, adventurous toddler. As a result of the cornucopia of intense medications, horrendous daily seizures, comas, and experimental surgeries, Harley's speech and movements are slow. Yet his witty personality peeks through. God has used him and my sister, to minister to so many people over the years, often through unwanted hospital stays and horrific experiences. Was Harley Claypool handcrafted by a loving God for a good purpose? He sure was! Has it been easy for my sister, a single mom? Absolutely not! But she clings to her heavenly Father, keeping her eyes on Him, so she can strive to remain unshaken and share Christ's love with everyone with whom she comes in contact.

....

God answers prayers in His perfect timing and in ways that will surprise and delight us so we'll know beyond a shadow of a doubt that He was the one who answered those prayers.

....

Another nephew, on my husband's side of the family, was born without a hip socket and with one leg shorter than the other. He has undergone several surgeries and wears a prosthetic leg. Yet he continues to persevere. In fact, I have never heard him complain about his leg. His freshman year in high school, Ethan was featured in a two-page spread in his school's yearbook with the title "Unbroken." The feature article, which hung at our county fair for all to see, says, "His belief in God has also given him hope in face of the challenges in life. 'I just know that God made me a special way and He has plans for me, and He's going to do good things with me,' de Neve said. 'That gives me peace of mind.'" What a testimony that has no doubt encouraged many more people than Ethan will ever realize.

The Provision of the Four Steps of Prayer

How does my family stand firm despite the ruckus waves that try to knock us down? By keeping our eyes on the Lord. That's why the first step of prayer is praise. It pries our eyes from our problems and puts them on the God who is more than capable of handling any situation. Only when we look at the big picture are we able to see how God might be using our difficult situation to shape us, direct us, and affect others for Him.

Shifting our focus from ourselves to our Creator is powerful on its own, yet the second prayer step is life-transforming. When we take time to confess sin to our Lord, invite Him to search our hearts, admit we're wrong, and ask for help to not commit that sin again, then we become clean vessels God can use in ways that we might not even realize while we're here on earth. Plus, when we have cleared the channel between ourselves and our heavenly Father, we can more clearly hear His promptings and be able to pray Holy Spirit–directed prayers. And, boy, does God love to answer those prayers!

The third step, thanksgiving, can change our whole demeanor. When we stop thinking of all the things annoying us and start thanking God for the many blessings He's given us to be thankful for, then our attitude will automatically change. (If you have trouble in this area, read Ann Voskamp's book *One Thousand Gifts*.)

When we have praised, confessed, and thanked, then our hearts are ready to intercede for others, asking God to intervene in their lives in powerful ways. Our prayers are often deeper and more powerful after we've spent time praising, confessing, and thanking. Then we're ready to do the work of the Holy Spirit, praying specifically and scripturally for those God brings to mind. Sometimes God will have us pray for people we don't even know—people we hear about on the news or on social media who are suffering. Both headline news alerts and Facebook posts provide a great opportunity to pray specifically for those who are hurting.

. . . .

Only when we look at the big picture are we able
to see how God might be using our difficult situation to shape us, direct us, and affect others for Him.

. . . .

Praying Continually

Although praying with others in one-accord, agreement prayer is a powerful way to keep us focused on each of the four steps and helps us intercede for others, that should not be the only time we pray the four steps of prayer. First Thessalonians 5:17 is an important two-word command: "Pray continually." If we truly want to remain unshaken in the craziness of life on earth, then we need to "pray continually." Besides, we want to experience God's perfect peace, don't we? And Philippians 4:4-7 gives us the recipe to receive His peace.

Rejoice in the Lord always. I will say it again: Rejoice!
Let your gentleness be evident to all. The Lord is near.

Do not be anxious about anything, but in every situation, by prayer and petition, with thanksgiving, present your requests to God. And the peace of God, which transcends all understanding, will guard your hearts and your minds in Christ Jesus.

Boy, do I love those verses! Sometimes we cling to our anxiety so strongly, but when we start with praise, by the time we get to confession we're usually ready to release the sin of worry to God and let Him fill us with His inexplicable peace.

I like to start my day with quiet time with the Lord, reading scriptures and praying. You might not be familiar with the term "quiet time." It's a special time between you and the Lord, when you can read and pray through the Scriptures, allowing the Holy Spirit to speak to your heart. This time also provides the perfect opportunity to pray both scripturally and specifically for others. Hand God your worries and let His peace and joy fill your heart.

I'm not a big fan of racing through the Bible in a year; I like to meditate on a passage. I might spend several days reading the same chapter each day so I can digest the meaning deeply and ask God to help me live out that passage. Sometimes I use my phone to snap a photo of the verses so I can review them throughout the day. Plus, I love finding wonderful nuggets of truth, wisdom, and direction to pray for others. The best scripture prayers come right out of our own quiet times. I like to stay flexible enough in my daily Bible readings that if God directs me to another passage for the morning, I'm not feeling stressed because I can't complete my scheduled reading.

Hand God your worries and let His
peace and joy fill your heart.

Where should you pray? Well, anywhere! Yes, I love praying in my quiet-time chair, but we're told to "pray continually." So where else can we focus on prayer? When I'm on the elliptical or taking the dogs for a walk by myself, the four steps of prayer provide a great way to help me refocus my mind—and stay focused on prayer. My son likes to pray through the four steps when he's riding his skateboard around his college campus.

Try this sometime: When you're driving alone (when my kids were little, that was a rare treat!), don't turn on the radio. Drive in silence, purposefully praying through the four steps of prayer and asking God to show you whom to pray for specifically. Sometimes He might direct you to a homeless man on the street, or a policeman in a squad car, or a woman with a carload of children so loud you can hear them through your closed windows. Or sometimes He'll choose your friend, spouse, or children. Being still allows the Holy Spirit to direct your prayers so you can pray for people you might not have thought needed God's intervention.

For each person reading this book, this is my prayer for you, directly from Ephesians 3:14-21.

> *For this reason I kneel before the Father, from whom every family in heaven and on earth derives its name. I pray that out of his glorious riches he may strengthen you with power through his Spirit in your inner being, so that Christ may dwell in your hearts through faith. And I pray that you, being rooted and established in love, may have power, together with all the Lord's holy people, to grasp how wide and long and high and deep is the love of Christ, and to know this love that surpasses knowledge—that you may be filled to the measure of all the fullness of God. Now to him who is able to do immeasurably more than all we ask or imagine, according to his power that is at work within us, to him be glory in the church and in Christ Jesus throughout all generations, for ever and ever! Amen.*

A Final Word from Sally

Dear reader, you are a child of the King of Kings and Lord of Lords (Revelation 19:16), the One who rules over all! Our King does as He pleases among the inhabitants of the earth (Daniel 4). It pleased God to create you in your mother's womb for His great purpose, which will make an impact on our world for Christ, glorifying God.

Psalm 139:13-14 says, "You created my inmost being; you knit me together in my mother's womb. I praise you because I am fearfully and wonderfully made; your works are wonderful, I know that full well." In the NASB, Psalm 139:13 says, "You formed my inward parts; You wove me in my mother's womb." The definition of the Hebrew word *yatsar*, the basis for the English word *formed*, means "pre-ordain, divine plan, purpose, form, fashion." Your DNA is special and created for your unique calling. God did not waste His breath when He made you! He has a unique, God-ordained purpose for each day of your life. He called you to Himself and filled you with the power of the Holy Spirit to fulfill His amazing calling on your life. Luke 24:49 says, "You are clothed with power from on high" (NASB).

If you're not sure if you're a child of God, please hear this: You *can* know for sure! In Romans 10:9 (NASB), God tells us, "If you confess with your mouth Jesus as Lord, and believe in your heart that God raised Him from the dead, you will be saved." You can pray a simple prayer like this: "Dear God, thank You for the gift of Your Son, Jesus. I believe He died on the cross for my sin. I desire to be Your child. Please forgive me of my sins and come into my heart. Thank You for hearing my prayer. In Jesus' name, amen." If you prayed this prayer, you belong to Him! John 1:12 says, "Yet to all who did receive him, to those who believed in his name, he gave the right to become children of God."

••••••••••••••••••••••••••••••••

If you're not sure if you're a child of God,
please hear this: You *can* know for sure!

••••••••••••••••••••••••••••••••

When Trials Threaten Your Foundation

Circumstances that can shake you are going to come your way. As we write this book, my family is experiencing an earth-shattering trial. You already read about my son David and his health crisis. That was last year. This year our eldest son, Ryan, was affected by a life-changing disease that was causing his body and mind to shut down. This young man loves Jesus and others, yet he was struggling so greatly that he couldn't even take care of himself. This not only affects him but his new wife and our whole family.

At first, it's natural to feel shattered when we face a crisis. Imagine with me seeing your beautiful, precious sons who loves Jesus and others so stricken with diseases. By God's grace and through years of remembering who God is, we put our eyes on Jesus, the author and finisher of our faith. He has called us and equipped us through prayer to fully run this race He has set before us. I hold on to the promise from Philippians 1:6: "Being confident of this, that he who began a good work in you will carry it on to completion until the day of Christ Jesus."

As I watch Ryan's siblings face their brother's illness, I see them coming around him and his wife, reminding them they're not alone. God and our family stand together with them as we go through this God-ordained trial. I give glory to God for their sibling bond and the encouragement they have for each other—a treasure such as God promises us even in dark places (Isaiah 45:3).

Some of the treasures have surprised me. Ryan is doing better now—walking and talking—and we can see that even in the broken state God was working through him. Ryan and I were together one day months after he was out of the hospital. We ran into a young man, and Ryan started up a conversation with him about his bike. I stepped back because I knew Ryan was going to share Jesus with him. About five minutes into the conversation, the young man's eyes grew big and he said, "I recognize you! You spoke with me a few months back at a restaurant." At that time Ryan could barely walk or talk, so both Ryan and I could only imagine what that conversation was like. Ryan smiled and said, "Did I say something like 'Jesus is Lord'?" The young man said, "Yes, and you said I should go to church. I have been going and I love it." Both Ryan and this young man were glowing with great joy. They continued talking for a few more minutes, and I stood there seeing that nothing is too hard and nothing is impossible for God.

After I shared about Ryan's situation at one of our "Unshaken" events, a precious mom wrote me. "Good Morning, Sally! I met you at the Moms in Prayer conference, and I also had met you years ago when my family attended Temecula Hills. I saw the beautiful cover picture of your family, and my heart melted. My youngest daughter has special needs and has been in various behavioral classes throughout the district. Year before last, she was in a class at a local elementary school, and she had this one aide in there whom she would talk about daily in deep adoration and excitement. She has always been very verbal about her love for Jesus and was usually shut down by staff because there were no other Christians in her class. This particular aide would share with her that he loved Jesus too, and he would smile at her and agree with her when she spoke about her love for Jesus. I would always pray for the teachers and aides and say a special prayer of thanks and protection over this particular aide. How amazing is it that this wonderful compassionate man that God put in my daughter's life for that season was your son Ryan! To me it is so precious! I got to witness the fruits of all the prayers over your son firsthand. Praying for your day and thanking God for you and your beautiful family!"

In the book of Acts, we see ordinary men who transformed a world because of their extraordinary God. In fact, they turned the world upside down for Christ, and their witness has changed lives for all eternity! In 2 Peter 3, Peter tells us to be holy (set apart) and godly (to worship well, live a life pleasing to God). Second Peter 3:17-18 says, "Therefore, dear friends, since you have been fore-warned, be on your guard so that you may not be carried away by the error of the lawless and fall from your secure position. But grow in the grace and knowledge of our Lord and Savior Jesus Christ. To him be glory both now and forever! Amen."

What's important to remember is that these words came from a man who was shaken when Jesus was arrested. In fact, Peter was so shaken he even denied he knew Christ! Later, he was shaken by his own failings. However, when he realized the depth of Christ's love for him, he renewed his commitment to the Lord, develop-ing a deeper loyalty to serve Him. Once he kept his eyes on Christ, Peter went on to be used by God in ways that were more than all he could have ever imagined. Peter went on to make an impact on the world for Christ—a world that was as dark and dangerous as it is today. The human race has forever been changed by the men and women who allowed God to empower them to stand unshaken in a shaken world.

Prayer is not simply an invitation to action; it's the invitation to a way of life. Each of the four steps of prayer is life-changing. You can become a woman of praise, of confession, of thanksgiving, and of intercession, resulting in being a woman who stands unshaken in this shaken world. Allow these four steps to change your life and experience God working through you powerfully.

Prayer is not just
an invitation to *action*;
it's the invitation to
a way of life.

Pressing On in the Unshaken Journey

Paul, a man of prayer, could have been easily shaken by the guilt of past murders, or by the agony over being flogged, beaten, imprisoned, shipwrecked, falsely accused, and facing impending death. Yet he was unshaken. He was a man of great joy, a man of great peace, a man of great prayer. In each of his letters, he shares the secret: He was continually abiding in Christ. Here are a few examples of his words of encouragement to you and me.

1 Corinthians 1:5

> In him you have been enriched in every way—with all kinds of speech and with all knowledge.

2 Corinthians 1:20

> No matter how many promises God has made, they are "Yes" in Christ. And so through him the "Amen" is spoken by us to the glory of God.

2 Corinthians 2:14

> Thanks be to God, who always leads us as captives in Christ's triumphal procession and uses us to spread the aroma of the knowledge of him everywhere.

Colossians 2:9-10

> In Christ all the fullness of the Deity lives in bodily form, and in Christ you have been brought to fullness. He is the head over every power and authority.

And, as it says in Philippians 1:6, God always completes what He has begun. What God says will happen does happen! Jesus completed with joy what God called Him to do on our behalf. Jesus was to live a sinless life, to willingly die for our sins and rise again, conquering sin and the penalty of death! Despite the complexity, the hardship, the impossibility of this calling, Jesus completed the race set before Him, victoriously declaring on the cross, "It is finished!" Jesus' work today is to complete God's will in us by working through us. We can get distracted on our way to fulfilling God's great calling. So, dear believers, we must keep our eyes on Jesus, stay in Him, and remain unshaken. This all happens through prayer.

The Legacy That Changes the World

I truly believe God has a great plan for this next generation. We have been praying in unified, powerful prayers for over 30 years. We are seeing God raise up an army of praying women, a mighty sisterhood to pray for this generation and the generations to come. Amazingly, this younger generation is joining us in those prayers! At our church recently, we had a concert of prayer. Many young people prayed alongside us for hours, crying out for the church, our city, and our country.

The mother of a young man named Nick Hall joined with other women to pray for him in a Moms in Prayer group. God is using this young man to make a difference with college students and others. Nick didn't set out to create the ministry PULSE; he set out to share the hope of Jesus on his college campus. But then so many people's lives were reached that PULSE was founded to help keep the message spreading. His organization recently held an event where nearly 500,000 people came together to stand for Jesus at the mall in Washington, D.C. Alongside Nick Hall and the young people of America stood Francis Chan, Dr. Tony Evans, Hillsong United, Josh McDowell, Jeremy Camp, and many others—standing for seven hours in unrelenting heat, praising God, and praying for our

country. Can you imagine what God will do as our young people stand together, unshaken for Christ? This is exactly what we're
asking God to do! May He empower this generation—and all the
generations until Christ returns—to walk powerfully before Him,
changing history.

One of our women came back from Cameroon, and she shared
this powerful story with me. As the bishop's wife was talking to a room
filled with praying women, she encouraged them and sent them forth
with this thought, "Don't ask what kind of Cameroon we will leave
this generation, but what kind of generation we will leave Cameroon."

May we ask ourselves what kind of generation will we leave this
land!

....

Can you imagine what God will do as our young
people stand together, unshaken for Christ?

....

Every day we're one day closer to seeing Jesus face-to-face. May
we live as Paul describes in Philippians 3:13-14: "One thing I do: forgetting what lies behind and reaching forward to what lies ahead, I
press on toward the goal for the prize of the upward call of God in
Christ Jesus" (NASB). Will your life make an impact on our world
for Christ? Will you keep your eyes always on the Lord? If you allow
Him, He will fulfill His great calling upon you and His great work
through you. Jesus tells us in John 15:7-8, "If you abide in Me, and
My words abide in you, ask whatever you wish, and it will be done
for you. My Father is glorified by this, that you bear much fruit, and
so prove to be My disciples" (NASB).

Will you keep your eyes on the Lord and keep Him at your right hand? If you do, you will not be shaken. Let us together make an impact on our world for Christ through prayer! May we live a life pleasing to Him, and may our lives bring glory to our heavenly Father as we stand together—unshaken.

Acknowledgments from Sally

I first thank God for His inexpressible gift of Jesus. I'm grateful for God's great calling to serve Him here and now, empowering every believer through the Holy Spirit for all we need for life and godliness.

I thank God for Fern Nichols and her answer to God's call upon her life to gather women together to pray for children and schools. Her life has had an impact on many for Christ. I am thankful for her continued mentorship and encouragement.

I thank the Lord for my dear friend Nancy McKenzie, who took me to my first Moms in Prayer meeting. And the amazing women of my Moms in Prayer group, Janet, Cathy, Lori, Jodi, Bonnie, Lynn, Carol, Dawn, Debbie, Remy, as well as our Grandmas in Prayer group.

Thank you to my world-traveling buddy, Marlae Gritter. Thank you, Estha Trouw for all the work and support to make this book possible. And thanks to my sisters at Moms in Prayer headquarters: Kelly Alarcon, Cathi Armitage, Susan Bagnell, Aubrie Burke, Rhonda Burt, Robin Clark, Sandra Chute, Kathryn Coffelt, Jill Farrell, Jackie Fitz, Judy Fuller, Sharon Gamble, Perri Houze, Kim Howard, Sue Iacoboni, Georgene Kamphuis, Jackie Marcum, Debbie Mears, Eileen Moore, Bonnie Nichols, Tiffany Nichols, Teresa Wu, and Linda Zifko.

I am thankful for my church, whose people live out God's Word and continue to offer support and encouragement. And for the women of our church who inspired me to write this book.

I thank the Lord for my sisters all over the world who stand with me in Moms in Prayer, fighting for children and schools.

Thank you, Stephen Kendrick, for inspiring me to write this book as you encouraged me and Estha at the *War Room* premier.

Cyndie, thank you for joining me in the journey of writing this book. You have made it fun and inspirational. May you continue to write; you are gifted.

My dear, precious family, how I thank the Lord for you: My husband, Ed, who continues to support me in so many ways. My children and their spouses, Ryan, Claire, Ginae, Garrett, David, Liz, and Aubrie, the reasons I began my journey of prayer. And for my grandchildren, Grant and Genevieve, the reasons I am so passionate to continue to pray until I am in heaven or the Lord returns. I love you more than words could express.

Acknowledgments from Cyndie

Thank you, Sally, for asking me to join you in this writing adventure. Helping women live out praise, confession, thanksgiving, and intercession is a game changer! I'm excited to see how God will use this book. Thank you, Estha Trouw, for helping us get off and running, and thanks to Pam Farrel and Teresa Evenson for your encouragement and wisdom.

Fern Nichols, thank you for starting Moms in Prayer International when I was just a teenager, and for the difference praying in a group has made in my life. And for every one of my prayer partners over the years who have prayed my kids through many and varied challenges, *thank you*! A special thanks to my daughter, Zoe, and her friends and their mothers who were willing to let me "try out" the Unshaken Bible Study on them: Becky and Mary Stokely, Karen and Kassandra Abirgas, Lisa and Jenna Merrill, and Cathy and Michelle Menconi. You were a fun group!

Of course, I am so grateful for my family, who has supported my writing endeavors all these years, and for my children, who have always allowed me to use their wacky antics as illustrations, especially when I was writing a newspaper column about family life. My husband, Marcel, and my two kiddos, Elliott and Zoe, always keep me laughing...and praying! My "momicita," Carol Claypool, deserves an award for not only keeping me breathing on several occasions, but for supporting and encouraging my writing since I was a little girl—and for collecting almost all my published articles since I was 12!

And a special thanks to my five siblings (as I am a proud "number four" of six): Cathy Chan, Cherrie Underwood, Colleen Claypool, Kelly Winter, and Cliff John Claypool. I wouldn't be me without you!

About Sally Burke

Sally Burke, president of Moms in Prayer International, grew up in Cocoa Beach, Florida. As a girl, she was fascinated with the space program and later became a space shuttle engineer. It wasn't until after she married and gave birth to her first two children that she and her husband came to faith in Christ and God began changing her priorities. Her introduction to Moms in Prayer International in 1990 was life-changing. As a young mom and a new believer, she discovered how faithfully God works in kids' lives in answer to prayer and the importance of the bond of sisterhood among praying moms. Compelled by joy, Sally began to share this hope with other moms.

God has led her step by step, first as a Moms in Prayer group leader and then as a Moms in Prayer area coordinator for her hometown, Temecula, California, where God raised up 60 new Moms in Prayer groups. She later became the regional coordinator for all of Riverside County and its 25 school districts with 700 schools and half a million students. In 2008 Sally "took on the world" for Moms in Prayer International as the director of field ministry, providing spiritual and strategic direction to the ministry worldwide. During her tenure, God doubled the number of nations where Moms in Prayer groups are found.

Today, in her role as president of Moms in Prayer International, Sally is carrying on the legacy begun over 30 years ago. She's a dynamic speaker and teacher who loves to encourage, equip, and empower women around the world in prayer. Sally has been interviewed on James Dobson's national radio program *Family Talk* as well as on *Today's Faith*, Calvary Chapel's national broadcast.

Sally and her husband, Ed, have four adult children—son Ryan married to Claire, daughter Ginae married to Garrett, son David married to Liz, and daughter Aubrie—and two grandchildren, Grant and Genevieve.

To contact Sally, email her at info@momsinprayer.org.

About Cyndie Claypool de Neve

Cyndie Claypool de Neve, who has an M.A. in Counseling Psychology, had her first article published in a national church publication at age 12. At 18 she started working in a newsroom and has written nearly 1000 articles, columns, and in-depth feature stories. She was the main editor and coordinator for the book *When Moms Pray Together*, published by Tyndale House in 2009, and was interviewed on James Dobson's international radio program, *Family Talk*.

As the director of communications at Moms in Prayer International for five years, Cyndie started the ministry's social media presence and initiated the use of video storytelling. To encourage moms to be praying daily, Cyndie coordinated the creation of the daily scripture prayers emailed to thousands of women every weekday morning. Cyndie also oversaw the organization's name change from Moms In Touch International to its current name, Moms in Prayer International, and helped establish the church-wide day of prayer, Bless Our Schools Sunday.

Today, she works as the senior director of creative and technical services at Emmanuel Faith Community Church, with about 4500 people attending on the weekends. She leads a department of nine, including staff in communications, graphics, video, media, and IT.

Passionate about prayer and helping people find their God-given purpose, Cyndie enjoys teaching and has led many Bible studies, prayer groups, workshops, and Sunday school classes.

Cyndie and her husband, Marcel, live in Escondido, California, where they have two creative and entertaining children—Elliott, who is in college, and Zoe, who is in high school—and three adorable rescue dogs.

To contact Cyndie, visit www.cyndiedeneve.com.

Moms in Prayer International

Are you a mom looking to pray one-accord, agreement prayers with another woman, as described by so many in this book? Do you want to bring your burdens for your children and their school to the Lord alongside another mom and experience God's inexplicable peace? A worldwide sisterhood of praying women is waiting for you to join them. Let us stand unshaken together and make a difference for Christ in our world!

Moms in Prayer International makes an impact for Christ on children and schools through prayer. Our vision is that every school in the world will be covered in prayer. For over 30 years God has been transforming lives as women gather together one hour weekly to pray in over 140 countries worldwide. We have witnessed revival and spiritual awakening. Women's lives are transformed as they pray these four powerful steps of prayer: praise, confession, thanksgiving, and intercession. A pastor in Nepal shared: "Moms in Prayer is spread all over the nations, and many pastors and leaders are demanding this movement in their areas and churches, because they experience that it is very powerful to change their children's lives and community as well."

Now you can attend *Unshaken* conferences where you will battle together with other moms in prayer and learn to stand unshaken despite your circumstances. Join a sisterhood of prayer warriors to impact the next generation for Christ.

For help finding another mom to pray with or to sign up to receive daily scripture prayers, visit:
www.MomsInPrayer.org

or contact us at
info@MomsInPrayer.org or (855) 769-7729

Find out which Moms in Prayer group type best fits your needs at
http://momsinprayer.org/get-involved/join-a-group/

Locate and register for an *Unshaken* event near you at:
http://momsinprayer.org/events/unshaken/

moms in prayer
I N T E R N A T I O N A L®
Praying for Children and Schools

Let's stand together—
unshaken and empowered through Christ.

Featured Ministries

Hearts at Home | www.heartsathome.org

Hearts at Home's mission is to encourage, educate, and equip every mom in every season of motherhood, using Christian values to strengthen families.

Young Life | www.younglife.org

Young Life reaches out to nearly 1.5 million middle school, high school, and college students in communities across the United States and around the world, providing role models, safe activities, and a sense of significance to these students.

Revive Our Hearts | www.reviveourhearts.com

Nancy DeMoss Wolgemuth has touched millions of women's lives through *Revive Our Hearts* and the True Woman Movement, calling them to heart revival and biblical womanhood.

MOPS | www.mops.org

Mothers of Preschoolers connects moms all over the world to a community of women, in their own neighborhoods, who meet together to laugh, cry, and embrace the journey of motherhood.

Love Wise | www.love-wise.com

Author and speaker Pam Farrel and her husband, Bill, help families love deeper so they can live better. They have dozens of books, including *The 10 Best Decisions Every Parent Can Make,* and resources filled with practical tips and encouragement available on their website.

Praying Life Foundation | www.prayinglife.org

The Praying Life Foundation offers in-depth seminars on prayer, keynote speaking, retreat formats, and so on. Jennifer Kennedy Dean is a significant voice in the current dialogue on spirituality and prayer. She's the author of numerous books on prayer and a popular speaker and conference leader.

Child Evangelism Fellowship | www.cefonline.com

CEF is a Bible-centered organization composed of born-again believers whose purpose is to share the gospel of the Lord Jesus Christ with boys and girls, and to disciple them in the Word of God and in a local church for Christian living.

Fellowship of Christian Athletes | www.fca.org

Fellowship of Christian Athletes is touching millions of lives, one heart at a time, as it challenges coaches and athletes on the professional, college, high school, junior high, and youth levels to use the powerful medium of athletics to change the world for Jesus Christ. FCA focuses on serving local communities by equipping, empowering, and encouraging people to make a difference for Christ.

Cru | www.cru.org

Cru (previously Campus Crusade for Christ International) helps to fulfill the Great Commission in the power of the Holy Spirit by winning people to faith in Jesus Christ, building them in their faith and sending them to win and build others; and helping the body of Christ do evangelism and discipleship.

Happy Home | www.arlenepellicane.com

Arlene Pellicane is a speaker and author of five books, including *Growing Up Social.* She has provided expertise as a guest on numerous television shows and radio programs.

Kendrick Brothers/War Room Movie | www.kendrick brothers.com

Kendrick Brothers Productions is the company founded by Alex and Stephen Kendrick that exists to honor Jesus Christ and make His truth and love known among the nations through movies, books, curriculum, and speaking. Their movies include *War Room*, *Courageous*, *Fireproof*, *Facing the Giants*, and *Flywheel*.

PULSE | www.pulsemovement.com

PULSE is a prayer and evangelism movement to empower the church and awaken culture to the reality of Jesus. It brings a fresh expression of Jesus to this generation with a voice and media that resonate with the youth culture.

Unshaken Study Guide

Strength and Encouragement
for Your Unshaken Journey

You have every reason to pray with confidence when you're praying to the God of the universe in accordance with His perfect will. Learn how to pray boldly and consistently in this companion guide to *Unshaken* by Sally Burke, president of Moms in Prayer International, and Cyndie Claypool de Neve.

Discover fresh insights into the art of prayer and entrust your family and future to the secure hands of Jesus as you explore—

Engaging questions
Recommended Scripture readings
Inspiring activities

Dig deep into this all-important study with a group or on your own, and get ready to see yourself and your world transformed.

To learn more about Harvest House books and
to read sample chapters, visit our website:

www.harvesthousepublishers.com

HARVEST HOUSE PUBLISHERS
EUGENE, OREGON